ITALIAN PARKS AND GARDENS

ITALIAN PARKS AND GARDENS

Massimo Listri   Cesare M. Cunaccia

RIZZOLI
NEW YORK

ACKNOWLEDGMENTS

Cesare Cunaccia wishes to thank the following people for their gracious assistance:

Cinzia Boscolo
Rosella Calnan
Luisa Cristiana Curti
Emilia Emo Capodilista
Giordano Emo Capodilista
Barnaba and Vittoria Ferruzzi Balbi
Dino Franzin
Paolo Genta Ternavasio
Franca Giacosa
Patrizia Lori
Costanza Massimo
Maria Consolata Morassutti Vitale
Guido Spanò di San Giuliano
Tessa Sperti Darin
Cristina Villoresi de Loche

First published in the United States of America in 1996 by
RIZZOLI INTERNATIONAL PUBLICATIONS, INC.
300 Park Avenue South, New York, NY 10010

First published in Italy in 1995 by
RCS Libri & Grandi Opere S.p.A., Milan

Copyright © 1995 RCS Libri & Grandi Opere S.p.A., Milan

Translation by Pierre Remords
Typesetting by Art Servizi Editoriali Srl, Bologne

ISBN 0-8478-1952-3
LC 95-72946

Printed and bound in Italy

Contents

To Gigi Bon, Friend

The Italian garden: places and symbols

Of all the colors green is the most beautiful, when it moves the soul of the onlooker who watches the spring germs sprout with new life, and rising high on their spikes as if they wanted to trample down death, they impetuously burst out all together, the very image of future resurrection.[1]

According to Rosario Assunto's aesthetic logic, the garden is an act through which thought becomes nature, and a mythical place of resurrection, a physically complete universe, and paradoxically, the space of an unending temporal dimension. As in Proust's *Recherche du Temps Perdu* (Remembrance of Things Past), the future occurs circularly, a perpetual returning of the past. The garden is "shaped nostalgia, and also implies a sentimental return to the Golden Days and a progression towards Utopia."[2] On the other hand—in extreme contradiction—it also conceals the germ of death, as can be gleaned from the myths in various cultures, from the biblical Garden of Eden to the Greek *gortos* of the Hesperides, and death always brings about palingenesis. In his *Invention of Mythology* Marcel Detienne upholds the theory that the word myth derives from a garden bearing this very name, built by the Syracusan tyrant Gelo in a decrepit trireme on the outskirts of the town.

There is a radical distinction between the *pardes*, the Mesopotamian paradise that idealizes the universe, a garden of delight and transcendence enclosing a temple, and the Greek *gortos*, walled-in and protected, which guards a secret awaiting disclosure, a treasure to be stolen, maybe forcibly, as Heracles did in the sacred garden of the daughters of Night. These two conceptions are synthesized in the biblical paradise on earth, where an ecstatic dimension of perfect and eternal bliss is countered by the mystery of its dissolution, and kept by a snake that recalls Ladon, the dragon who watched over the apples of the Hesperides.

Built by the great architect Daedalus for King Minos of Crete, the Labyrinth is another canonical place for a mystery journey: its confusing network of paths and passageways conceal the Minotaur, the monster begotten by Pasiphae and the white bull sent from the sea by Poseidon. This time, astuteness is required to enter and, above all, proceed backwards towards safety. The labyrinth as a metaphor is ambiguous and prismatic: this dangerous journey towards an obscure epicenter (a journey from which one might not return) may symbolize torment or solace, perdition or purification. For King Solomon, in the Hebrew cabala, the labyrinth may represent the direction of a journey towards some alchemic sublimation. When it is designed in inlaid stones on the floors of medieval cathedrals built between the Romanesque and the gothic period, it alludes to the progress towards redemption and the pilgrimage to earthly and heavenly Jerusalem. Embroidered on the jerkin of the young and melancholy gentleman portayed by Bartolomeo Veneto in the sixteenth century, the labyrinth reveals an inner mood of anxiety and indecision. It appears that the topiary labyrinth, very fashionable in the mannerist and baroque periods, entered the garden poetics as early as the fourteenth century. But, as Lionello Puppi remarks, "in its

comprehensive consistency, the garden itself is a labyrinth or, better still, the representation of an inner and secret 'history', serving and expressing itself as a complement or an alternative to the 'real' outside and written history, although [the garden] is incapable of being an aim or a conclusion. . . . The garden as the labyrinth of history."[3]

Another cornerstone in the history of gardens is Arcadia, an oneiric land of charms encased between high mountains and through which winding brooks meander, a land with no spatial boundaries, and free from the control of the pantheistic god who permeates every creature living there. A place of appeasing serenity, of peaceful, estranging sleep, it is inhabited by idealized shepherds like Virgil's Titiro, who spend more time singing to the sound of the flute and dancing than watching over their herds. However there is deceit even there, where Narcissus drowns, attracted by the reflection of his own image in one of the many sources of the Helicon. A place of complete harmony between human beings, natural lymphs, and gods, Arcadia is an artificial, sophisticated mimesis of nature, permeated with the nature's very precariousness, and ultimately becomes the metaphorical manifestation of the yearning for a golden age. With Zeus's birth sprouts the seed of the end of mankind's happiest period. The succession of the seasons, which originates in the silvery period inaugurated by the god's birth, clearly indicates the apparition of Time, with all its dramatic and devastating effects. As Lévi-Strauss pointed out, *Et in Arcadia ego*, the symbolic and ambiguous title of the two famous paintings by Guercino and Poussin, becomes a sort of *memento mori*, to warn us that even in the suspended, happy world of Arcadia, death is omnipotent. A pagan place if ever there was one, Arcadia springs up again among the ruins of classicism during the Renaissance. The sixteenth century Venetian painters transpose the fertile, peaceful, local landscape into a gratifying, sunlit spaciousness—yet another reflection of the lost Arcadian Eden. From the crystallized pictorial experiments of the Fontainebleau school, through the newly-recovered and composed ranks of the seventeenth-century painting schools of Emilia (especially Albani, thanks to Poussin's and Lorrain's absolute, perfect icons) this paradise-land is still celebrated in the eighteenth century by Watteau's grace and by Hubert Robert's early-romantic suggestions.

Christian ideology also projects into the garden its longing for the lost paradise, as well as the utopian image of the heavenly kingdom. It is no mere chance that the Bible tells that the risen Christ—whose sepulchre was indeed in a suburban garden—appeared to Joseph of Arimathaea in the guise of *hortolanus*. The medieval *hortus conclusus*, deriving from the Arab garden and imported to Europe at the time of the crusades in the Holy Land, was a place for the contemplative soul to be nourished by the desire for cosmic improvement, and was the ideal association of paradise lost and promised. According to the precepts in Pietro de' Crescenzi's treatise, the *hortus* is strictly divided into orchard, meadow, and *viridarium* (garden), with a fountain of thaumaturgic waters in its center. Revolving around the legend of the source of life and eternal youth, the *hortus* is often a metaphor for the Christ or the Holy Mother, and becomes a place for a highly-needed mental escape. Separated from the teeming, malodorous substance of the swarming medieval town, a place of anger, a chaotic furnace where the devastation of time is consumed, the *hortus* is a protected microcosm, whose high walls—more than a physical boundary—seem to symbolize the reification of eternity. Its theorization by Alberto Magno[4] as a concretization of the idea, according to the double religious and erotic line of medieval Platonism, exemplifies the absolute beauty of an uncorrupted nature, free from the ravages of passing time. Thus it seems death cannot take root inside this garden, and the crude reality of recurring wars and plagues sinks into a very sweet oblivion. From the *Songe du Verger* to Guillaume de Lorris's *Roman de la Rose*, corroborated by Petrarch's early-humanistic ideals, this utopia of the healing garden was to find its best representation in Boccaccio's *Decameron*, in a very profane, hedonistic, and erotic interpretation: the garden constitutes a frame for the narration, a guideline along which this complex work is structured.

For at least two centuries, the estranging, cathartic dreams of the medieval man were to remain prisoners of this imaginary heritage. In the fifteenth century, colored enamel emphasized the greenness of a meadow on Louis d'Anjou's golden cup; on the duke of Berry's tapestries could be seen oranges, chestnuts, oak trees, and pine trees, under which vibrated the shady presence of wild animals, just as in the miniatures of the *Très Riches Heures*. The pleasant garden strewn with flowers serves as a background for Stefan Lochner's, Stefano da Zevio's, and Pisanello's elegant courtly madonnas, for the rhapsodic dance of Jan Van Eyck's Blessed in his *Adoration of the Lamb*, and during the humanistic period, for the extremely Thomistic radiance of Fra Angelico's paintings. In his *Triptych of Delights* Bosch was the only one who dared contaminate the courtly, sacred dimension of the *hortus* with the domination of chaos, expressed by a polymorphic proliferation of monstrous but nevertheless alluring creatures.

In this confrontation between man and nature, the garden appears as an unnatural event, since its existence connotes modeling, transforming, and substituting, in which constancy and variation are the two unescapable laws. Constancy is embodied in the trees and shrubs, while variation is rendered by the passing of the seasons, the changes in color and growth.

Kant is not so far from the idealistic essence of humanism when, in his *Critique of Judgment*, he defines the garden as "an Art that consists in disposing nicely the products of Nature, to express aesthetic ideas according to the analogy of language." Thus the Renaissance garden is always supported by strict iconographic planning, drawn up by men of letters or other eminent cultural representatives of that period. No longer a place of mysticism for erotic or religious escape, it becomes man's proper place, inasmuch as the man uses this dimension—now professedly secular—to create a perfect space, organized in accordance with the divine laws governing the universe. Thus it is practically always planned along a single, central vista, and those who follow this itinerary— punctuated by the symbolic presence of statuary, where classic and Christian culture mingle in harmonious dialectics—are able to elevate

and educate their minds and souls. It is no longer necessary to separate the garden from the outside world: the mathematical order with which it is organized permeates everything around it, and every foreshortening is visually inserted in the constraining meshes of this perspective grid.

The true manifesto of the garden conceived as organized landscape—an archetype where man, exerting his own control over nature, takes on the part of demiurge—is Francesco Colonna's *Hypnerotomachia Poliphyli*, printed in 1499 in Aldo Manuzio type (Venice). The substantially artificial conception of the Renaissance garden finds there its highest exemplification, in the description of three exquisite gardens respectively made of glass, silk, and precious stones. But even the Renaissance prototype of earthly paradise is weakened by the threat of human transitoriness. Botticelli alludes to it in his *Spring*, in which the solar iconographic program seems somewhat obscured in Proserpine's face which, rather than appearing regenerated in her guise of life herald, seems still darkened by the shadows of Hades. And her lips, turned almost colorless by her long stay in the netherworld, seem to shape silently Lorenzo's verses: "However beautiful youth may be, it will disappear: the morrow holds no certainties."[5]

With the waning of the radiant certainties of the Renaissance ideal, the tragedy of lost control over the world, and the theoretical defeat of the neoplatonic conception, nature reconquers its matter and pulsations and for the first time becomes sole protagonist. With its mysterious caves and riverbeds that seem to live a life of their own, like the forest in Shakespeare's *Macbeth*—its dark, tortuous ravines where Medusa might be hiding, its steep, "gothic" rock work—the mannerist garden baffles its visitor with all sorts of surprises and metaphysical tricks. Alarming automatons, perspectives that are swollen or contorted, vertiginous, oppressing gullies, mysterious nymphaeums, gigantic creatures, cosmological hints, esoteric arcana, a whole repertoire borrowed from the wonderful world of the *Wunderkammer* composes an endless hymn to metamorphosis. The luminous certainty of the Renaissance axial vista has disappeared, to be replaced by the dramatic force of chiaroscuro, which helps to devise sinuous itineraries, no longer meant to educate but to confuse both senses and mind by the spell they cast.

"And the sudden water is carried downwards, / the Water that from a beautiful brook turns into a mountain stream."[6] Armida's garden makes extensive use of water, present in a thousand different forms, like a magic philtre that works the innumerable seductions of enchantment. But the nature of the mannerist garden—apparently dominated by monsters populated by the sleep of reason—also functions as an exorcist because of its hyperbolic essence, the multiplication of the narrative themes of its decoration. As Manfredo Tafuri remarks, the mannerist artist:

> no longer has a universal and solid ground on which to mirror himself, and all he can do is jump over the obstacle, take possession of the laws that govern the infinite fermentation of manner, confine himself to remaining a disillusioned experi-

menter while performing complicated operations bordering on magic and exorcism. . . . When one is afraid of something he feels like a constant menace, his very first impulse is to absorb what frightens him and exhibit it, in order to exorcise it.[7]

These are some of the salient places and stages in the development of Italian garden history. With the international climate of the Fontainebleau school, leavens were to spread throughout Europe and play a decisive part in the creation of national garden cultures. The Leibnitzian period of the French baroque, and English landscape gardening, with William Kent and his followers, were to bring new values to the Italian poetics. Sown with such fertile suggestions as those of Henry Cocker and mainly Russell Page, as well as Carlo Scarpa's Zen-inspired oriental evocations, this furrow is still alive with creativity. Characterized by a soothing, well balanced, humanistic geometry, this calling has found in Pietro Porcinai its most extraordinary songster.

Cesare Cunaccia and Elena Barbalich

1. From Ugo da San Vittore, *Eruditiones Didascalicae*, XII.
2. O. E. Torsten - C. F. Schroder, *Garden Architecture in Europe*, Cologne 1991.
3. L. Puppi, *Il terzo nome del gatto*, Venice 1989.
4. Alberto Magno, *De laudibus Beatae Mariae Virginis*, I. XII. C. I, "De Horto concluso", in *Opera omnia*, vol. XXVI.
5. Lorenzo de' Medici, *Il trionfo di Bacco e Arianna*.
6. T. Tasso, *Gerusalemme liberata* (Jerusalem Delivered), C. XVIII, ott. XXI.
7. M. Tafuri, "Il mito naturalistico nell'architectura del Cinquecento," in *L'Arte*, n.s., I, 1968.

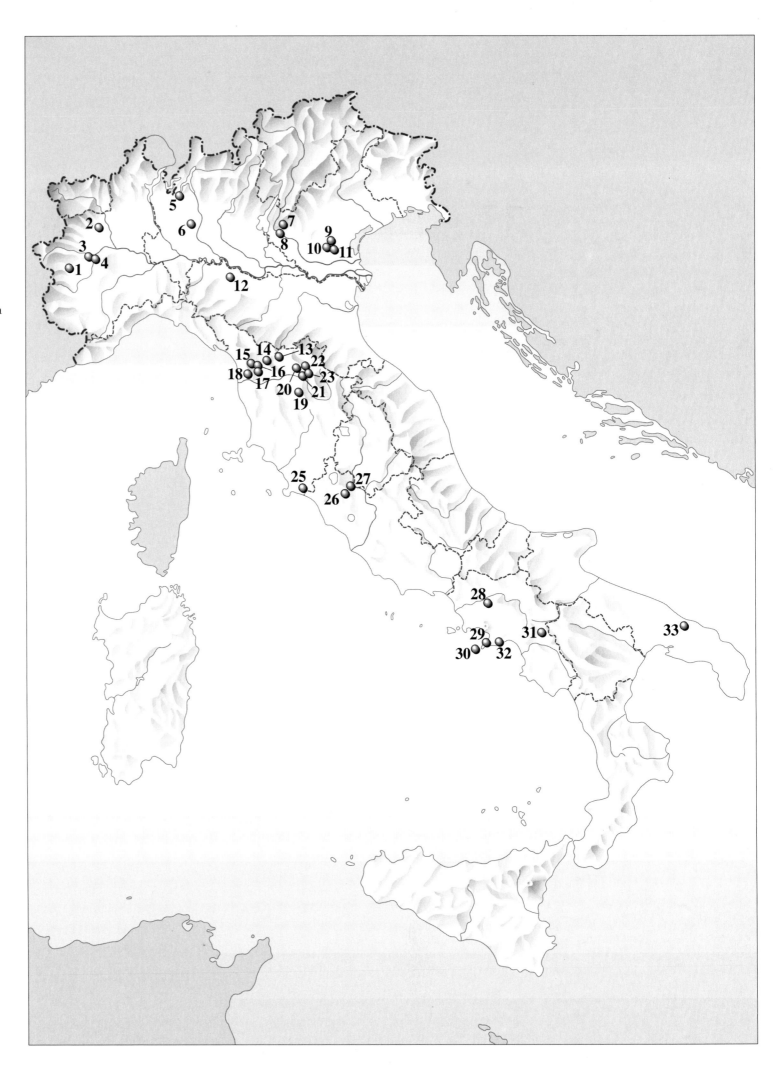

The Parks and Gardens

Villa Agnelli
Villar Perosa (Turin)

Not far from the unruly growth of the city of Turin, and its hills disfigured by neglected or parcelled-out parks, whole stretches of landscape are hidden away, landscape gardens where "the idea of beauty can be isolated and set off by choosing the best of natural shapes."

Spring diversifies this greenness with the blossoms of the almond, peach, apple and cherry trees, and you can see white and pink patches and whole snowy rows interspersed with the blondness of the first poplar leaves sprouting from their buds.

Barbara Allason's words ring nostalgically in her book *Old villas, old hearts*, in which she describes, in the first years after World War II, the still-intact beauty of the hills near Turin, the "true miracle of beauty and fullness of light" that had moved Friedrich Nietzsche in 1888.

The garden of Villa Agnelli, at Villar Perosa in Val Chisone, is organized around an eighteenth-century church inspired by Filippo Juvarra's church on nearby Monte Superga, and meant to give "a classical tone on the urban, familiar horizon of the hills." Although abounding with echoes and historical memories, the garden can be considered an authentic elaboration of modern times.

In 1955 Marella Agnelli commissioned Russell Page to restructure what had become a typical, picturesque nineteenth-century park—eclectic, but deprived of any typological or aesthetic identity. No systematic plan had been devised to check the domestic disorder of colorful flowerbeds and the proliferation of a great variety of trees, or to give a precise reason to the ornamental lakes that casually interrupted the vegetation. Page—the guru of contemporary gardening, upholder of a clear, geometric stamp more akin to Le Nôtre's eighteenth-century rigor than to Gertrude Jekyll's florid style—set to work, and Villar Perosa became a place of highly versatile experimentation. But Page never forgot the austere eighteenth-century façades of the villa, indented with low, elegant porticos, almost immune to the passing of time with their symbolically sober character.

The walls of the villa enclose a vivid portion of Piedmontese history. The villa may have been built for Victor Amadeus II of Savoy, a great condottiere responsible for the new importance of the House of Savoy on the European political stage. His image appears three times inside the villa, as a portrait, a bust, and a medallion. According to the first unquestionable documents dating from the end of the eighteenth century, the villa became part of the possessions of Count Piccone, governor of Asti, then passed on to the Gambas and the Turinettis. Yielding very little to rococo grace, its austere appearance suggests its original function as a place of recreation and refreshment for the soldiers stationed in the neighboring fortifications of Assietta, built to protect the frontier against the menacing French. This perhaps explains why the villa attracted the notice of one Agnelli, who was an officer posted in the fortified town of Pinerolo. After renting the villa beginning in 1811, he finally bought it in 1853. From that time, with its exquisitely Piedmontese character in which the graceful patterns of the rococo stuccos mingle with archi-

tectural traces of Juvarra's repertoire and rarefied chinoiseries, the villa has become the privileged place for the Agnellis' public and private life.

In order to restore an eighteenth-century character to the villa, whose appearance was well matched with the classical taste that presided over garden landscaping, Russell Page set aside his initial architect's visions and endeavored to give the garden more open and essential spaces, plenty of sunlight, and a great cohesion with the landscape in which it is immersed. Thus the frame of vegetation underlines the presence of the neighboring hills and meadows, as well as the slight, soft curve of the church dome, a part of Juvarra's massive structure floating in the distance.

The various levels that compose the park have been subdivided by the graphic geometry of rose beds, which burst out into the very romantic, apparent disorder of blossoming magnolias, 'Exbury' azaleas, rhododendrons, *Scilla nonscripta* and *Convallaria*, whose colors fill the slope between the terraces and the little stream running in the valley bed. As always in Page's creations, his close relationship with the client, in this case Marella Agnelli, proved fundamental: the latter made very precise suggestions and helped Page understand the spirit of the place. The garden's total integration with the surrounding landscape is entirely intentional and contradicts Page's usual predilection for Hidcote Park, Lawrence Johnston's masterpiece in Gloucestershire, England, which deliberately ignores an uninteresting landscape.

Little by little the rhythm imparted to the park unravels, breathes, pursues its descending course in the blooms of *Lythrum, moyesii* and *hugonis* roses, *Iris siberica, Spiraea cantoniensis*, and *Hemerocallis*. The park is a sort of musical adagio, accompanied by the bass-notes of a brook whose pace Page has checked in increasingly larger lakes that regulate its slow, comforting Arcadian cadence. An Eden rich with ancient prestige, the garden's sober, elegant character seems to be allegorically embodied in a statue of Diana the Huntress standing out against the strict hedges of the last terrace. The dynamic rotation of Diana's typically eighteenth-century posture encompasses the surrounding vales with a sense of chaste dominion.

Created in 1955 by Russell Page for Marella Agnelli, the Villar Perosa park surrounds the villa, a sober eighteenth-century building.
Following pages: After the initial geometric rhythm, the garden unfolds in a romantic crescendo, a colorful world composed of magnolias, 'Exbury' azaleas, rhododendrons, Scilla nonscripta, and irises.

Previous pages: Russell Page has domesticated the brook in increasingly larger basins that punctuate the Arcadian cadence of the park.

Particularly congenial with Page's poetics, the formal features of the eighteenth-century gardens are generated by the volumes of the topiary art, and the pattern of the geometric rose beds.

*This lawn features geometric hedges and
trees in a real display of topiary art.
Opposite: A few suggestive views
of various parts of the garden.*

Ronchi Farmstead
Aglié (Turin)

The hedge seemed to form a row of chapels that disappeared under the expanse of their flowers, shaped like so many altars; under them, the sun cast a checkboard of light on the ground, as though shining through a stained-glass window; their perfume radiated just as unctuously, was just as circumscribed in its shape, as if I had been standing in front of the Holy Mother's altar.

The rose garden of the Ronchi farmstead, created on an old vegetable garden dating from the beginning of the century, seems to have been created to surround its visitor with a secret aura, a sort of protected, exclusive refuge, in the very space woven with light and shade, and heady fragrances described by Marcel Proust in the above passage from *Remembrance of Things Past*. Surrounded on every side by a high hedge of red *Pyracantha*, with a counterpoint provided by the infinite chromatic gradations of the profusion of roses, the rosery is closed by two sturdy gates, just like the pleasant garden of the *Roman de la Rose*. Two side alleys, whose progress is marked by a succession of arches, are drowned beneath the many-colored screen of climbing roses, interwoven with the rising polyphony of clematis, slender *Delphinium* and althaea. Digitalis, peonies, irises, lupins, violets, and tender nineteenth-century dwarf carnations flower from spring to autumn, according to the species. The Parma violets and pansies, that grow in fragrant patches on the green grass, form a velvety background for this luxuriant exuberance.

In his water-colors, Pierre-Joseph Redouté, called the Raphael of Roses, seems to express his anxious solicitude for his fleeting madonnas, the roses, some belonging to long-forgotten species (or if still known, they bloom secretly, in some ancient provincial garden), for once the floriculturists have created a new type of rose, they are not concerned about its permanence but merely use it to create a new race.

Here, in this corner of Piedmont, Mario Praz's words are belied: even Redouté, who immortalized over a thousand specimens, would be astonished by the incredible variety of roses collected by the proprietors of the Ronchi farmstead: four hundred and fifty different species. With infinite passion and patient philologic research in specialized nurseries in England and France, in forgotten gardens or in neglected, weed-grown Italian vegetable gardens, the couple of proprietors (who have also conceived this rosery) have composed a flower mosaic that would be the envy of such historic collectors as Maria Feodorovna, Empress of Russia, who conceived the Pavlovsk Rose Pavillion, or Joséphine de Beauharnais of Malmaison.

A host of these ancient roses have, little by little, replaced the initial modern roses, led by the secular beauty of 'Alba' and 'Centifolia', perfumed and swollen with delicately hued pastel petals, or varieties with evocative names like 'Cuisse de Nymphe Emue', dating from 1797, or 'Félicité Parmentier', with its flat, pale pink petals, or 'Celestial' (1739), whose tender corolla exquisitely matches the greyish-green leaves. Here is also 'hugonis' and 'Duchesse d'Angoulême', created in 1827 during the Restoration and dedicated to Louis XVI's daughter, and the musky fragrances of 'Felicia' and 'Fantin-Latour', named after the painter. Sumptuous in glowing crimson variegated with violet, 'Cardinal de Richelieu' stands out—the rose that was created when Dumas's three musketeers were a great hit. The predominant yellow of 'Gruss an Aachen's' double flowers (created in 1909) blends with 'Village Maid's' white streaked with pink, with the nineteenth-century grace of 'Comte de Chambord', and the white, exceptionally fragrant opulence of 'Madame Hardy', the famous damask rose created in 1832, probably the most perfect of its type. The story of 'Purezza' is more recent: a cultivar obtained by Quinto Mansuino in the 1950s by crossbreeding *Rosa chinensis* 'Minima' with *Rosa banksiae* 'Lutea', a creeper with immaculately white, fragrant double flowers. It has grown so rapidly, twined around the tangle of an unusual deep lilac wisteria, that it has covered the southern façade of the old farmhouse, turning it into an impressionist image.

By now almost too small to contain the swelling tide of roses, this wonderful rosery is set in a garden divided into two vast terraced zones and a meadow, watched over by tall trees against whose background stand yet other enormous rose bushes. The proprietors' virtuosity in creating this botanical collection seems incredible; they came from Turin only fifteen years ago, and, little more than amateurs, without any help whatsoever, devoted themselves to their creation. Their talent is also evident in the wide range of species that populate the Ronchi farmstead. *Camellia japonica*, hydrangeas, jasmines, viburnums, lilacs, lilies of the valley, and rhododendrons make up a palette that confirms the intimate, nineteenth-century aura of this happy place. Here, even the slow growth of *Parrotia persica* and *Osmanthus* seems to quicken, in order to take part in the choral outburst of life, encouraged or checked by the owners' care, errors, conquests, and discoveries. The gardens give a continuous show, with a climax in May-June, dominated by the rose, the flower with infinite symbolic meanings. This is a garden that thoroughly conveys Gertrude Stein's famous words, "a rose is a rose, is a rose, is a rose."

In this corner of the garden, roses grow among the lavandas and foxgloves. Following page: A stone-paved alley is bordered by rose bushes, among which are 'Princess of Nassau', 'Gloire de Dijon', 'Cardinal de Richelieu', 'Salet', and 'Félicité Perpetue'.

*Previous page: Views of the garden.
Above: A floral foreground of Digitalis
purpurea and Lonicera x Brownii.
Opposite: 'Ballerina' roses in full bloom.*

Villa d'Aglié-Giacosa
Turin

Do you know Turin? It is the kind of city I like, the one city I love in fact. Calm, almost majestic. A perfect place for strolling and contemplating (thanks to its beautiful pavement and a yellow-orange tonality in which everything is blended). A pleasant eighteenth-century fragrance. And how eloquent the palaces are to our senses: quite different from the Renaissance castles! . . . The atmosphere is dry, sublimely transparent, I would never have thought light could make a city so beautiful.

This is what Friedrich Nietzsche wrote in a letter to the musicologist Carl Fuchs in April 1888. The city with which the philosopher had fallen in love, and whose eighteenth-century grace he praises so passionately in this letter, is obviously not the present Turin. Concrete has attacked the historical patrimony of the villas and parks on the hills in a merciless battle which Fruttero and Lucentini superbly described in *La donna della domenica* ('The Sunday Woman'), the exceptional novel they wrote in 1972. However, a few pieces of the historic mosaic have survived, and bear witness to the magnificence of Carlo di Castellamonte and Filippo Juvarra's Turin, which was begun by Victor Amadeus II and completed by a patrician society "that built the villas always further into the hills," towards Juvarra's Superga Basilica, "an element of distant vision, a focal point on the new border of the city," in Andreina Griseri's words.

Among the hills that rise above the plain of the Po river, in a place with a commanding view over the city of the House of Savoy, stands Villa d'Aglié. Retracing the villa's life through the succession of its owners amounts to leafing through some of the most salient pages of Piedmontese history.

In 1610, the villa belonged to Duke Charles Emmanuel I; two years later it was bought by Bellezia, a jurisconsult, Emmanuel's treasurer and mayor of Turin, who was to build the first proper garden. In the great building fever of the first years of the eighteenth century, immediately after the siege and the victory of the House of Savoy, the house itself was substantially transformed, taking on its present aspect, with a façade marked off by a double gallery.

Towards the middle of the eighteenth century the villa was given the name Castelmagno by its new proprietor, Count Ignazio di Castelmagno, who would strew the garden with marble statues and busts. Finally, near the end of the century, the villa became a part of the possessions of Benedetto Maurizio of Savoy, Duke of Chiablese and Aglié, and last-born son of King Charles Emmanuel II, who gave it the name it bears today. In 1820 the villa was bought by the British ambassador Sir John Foster, who transformed the strict Italian-style gardens into a romantic, English-style park, introducing rare varieties of trees, including horse-chestnuts, Lebanon cedars, and sequoias, and enriching the "wilderness" that encloses the park like the wings of a stage, with hornbeams and yews. From the middle of the nineteenth century until 1928, the villa was inhabited by the marquesses Pilo Boyl di Putifigari.

After first belonging in 1610 to Duke Charles Emmanuel I of Savoy, the villa became property of the Count of Castelmagno, who dotted the gardens with marble busts and sculptures; then it passed over to Benedetto Maurizio of Savoy, Duke of Chiablese and Aglié, whose name it still bears today.

But despite a few insignificant modifications of its gardens during the war, the true turn in Villa d'Aglié's history was to be given in 1958 by the English gardener Russell Page, who restructured the space in front of the villa. Page's striking intervention bears a fair resemblance to a drawing on a 1790 cadastral register, which was discovered in an antique library, as if confirming the intuition of a man who, like Le Nôtre, delighted in modeling the landscape, subverting levels, composing straight water-courses, and making canals flow into vast ornamental lakes.

On the right side of the vast lawn stretching in front of the villa, the elegant, airy, geometrical composition of the four rectangular flowerbeds filled with roses, parallel to the box hedge, is balanced by the Lebanon cedar, a remnant of Sir John Foster's romantic experiments, and converses with the *Sequoia sempervirens*.

On the left of the building, the small lawn is lorded over by an ancient *Liriodendron tulipifera* and a tall *Tamarix japonica*, silhouetted against a border of 'Nevada' roses and white peonies.

In spring and throughout the summer, the upper courtyard, which gives access to the wood that surrounds the house, is decorated with large tubs of lemon trees. The ancient semicircular flower boxes brim with flowers, generally in shades of pink to match the pale brick-color of the eighteenth-century walls.

It seems that at Villa d'Aglié, nothing can perturb the exquisite, suspended balance between green spaces, flowers, and tall trees. It is such a perfect harmony, veiled with a sweetly melancholy note, as though the Marschallin in Richard Strauss's *Rosenkavalier* might suddenly appear. This was achieved through the collaboration of the owner, Franca Giacosa, and Russell Page—a man who is undoubtedly one of the greatest landscape gardeners of our time, an Englishman with a passion for Louis XIV's France, a gardener who, paradoxically, never had a garden of his own.

The owner's continuous input is perceptible alongside Russell Page's design; for many years Franca Giacosa has been devoting all her love and infinite energy to her garden.

A tall Tamarix japonica, an ancient Liriodendron tulipifera, some Lebanon cedars, sequoias, horse chestnuts, hornbeams, and yew trees grow together in the "wilderness" that surrounds the park.

In front of the building are four rectangular rose beds, outlined by box hedges. A century-old Lebanon cedar partly conceals the villa.

Following pages: Russell Page, perhaps the greatest contemporary landscape gardener, has reintroduced a sophisticated eighteenth-century French note in the area in front of the villa.

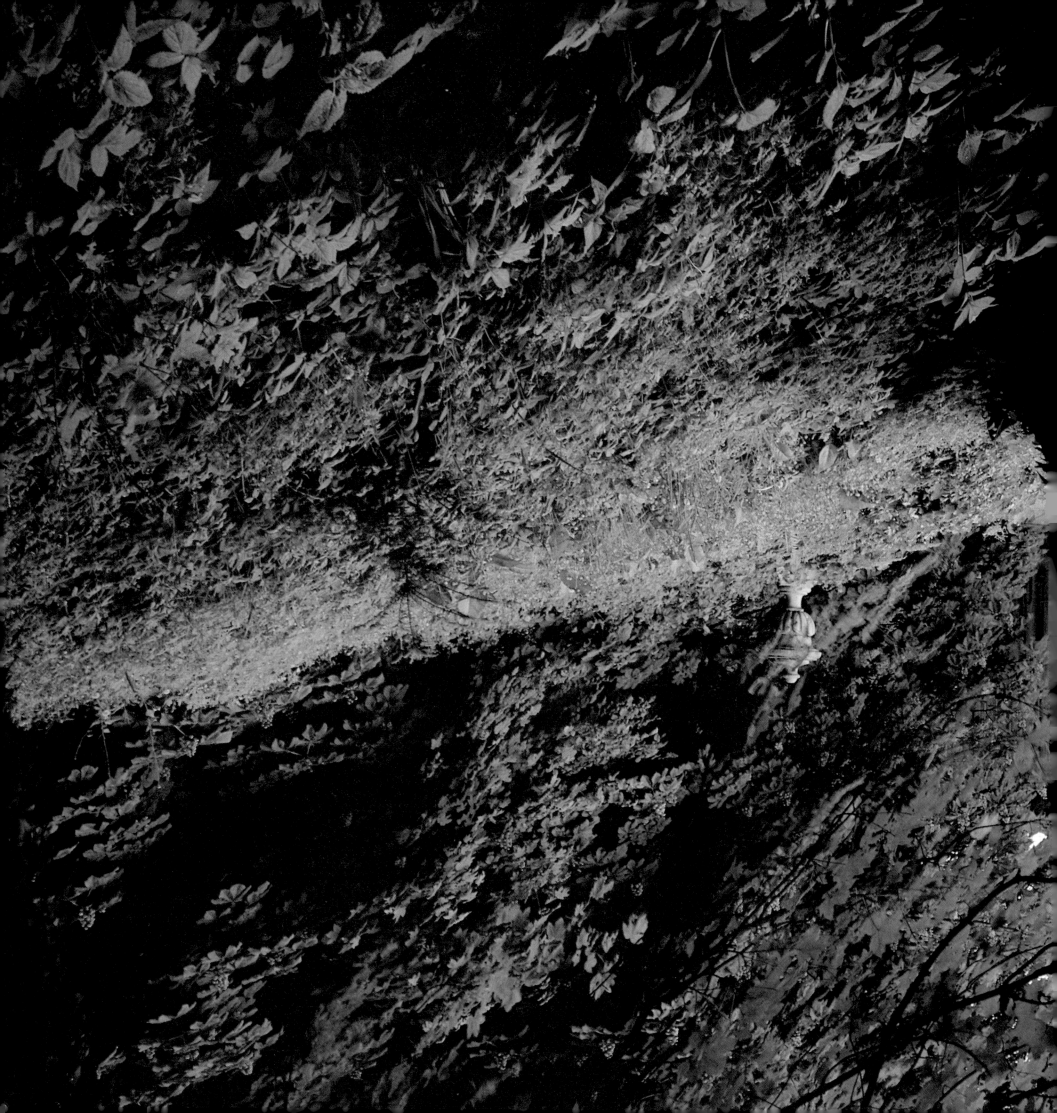

Genta Ternavasio Garden
Turin

It seems easy when you say it, but I defy the Italians to make English landscape gardens. The temperature of the ground and the heat of the sun deprive them of a pleasant variety of tone, of color. . .

This statement by the Prince of Ligne—as usual a sharp and polemical adversary of Italian culture—is contradicted by the essentially English organization of a garden created by Paolo Genta Ternavasio in the Piedmontese countryside.

The garden and park are built on the site where, at the beginning of the seventeenth century, stood the convent of Saint Francis. The present buildings were erected in the eighteenth century. Two long wings at right angles enclose the inner garden, a kitchen garden, and a graveled area, while a smaller building, separated from the main structures, faces the vast park. There is strong feeling of fusion between the buildings and gardens. In addition to the long canal, which marks the boundaries of the park, a tree-surrounded meadow becomes an essential element in the park's relationship with the surrounding countryside. With its regular layout and an intentional feeling of closeness, the kitchen garden, a real *hortus conclusus* enclosed by a brick wall with a single neogothic archway, recalls the ancient garden of the convent. In the inner garden, the verticality of the tall fir trees is underlined by wisterias. When they bloom in spring, the tender mauve of their flowers mingles with the dark green of the trees.

Paolo Genta's garden and park are clearly inspired by a fundamental Englishness, confirmed by the rustic, dry stone walls; the grass and brick paths; the ancient, creeping roses; the mixed border; the thick hedges, some of which are fancifully clipped; the presence of water; and the apparently irregular tree plantings. The so-called pagoda—a small, hexagonal brick temple with a copper-decked cupola, a discreet quotation from the local eighteenth-century glossary—seems almost suspended above the waters of a small lake dotted with waterlilies, against a background of oaks, lime trees, white poplars, and small cypresses (for the Chinese touch). This taste for chinoiseries, reinvented by Genta with a particularly elegant stamp, was a true leitmotiv of the Piedmontese Rococo, seen in such masterpieces as the paintings for the drawing-rooms of the Queen's Villa in Turin, done by Pietro Massa and Fariano around 1755.

The garden's British influence is mitigated by a certain Age of Enlightenment rationalism, which finds its expression in the geometric cut of the box and yew hedges, and the stereometric plan of the labyrinth, built on a rectangular surface patterned with green "walls" and brick paths. This labyrinth is designed to enable meetings between people, rather than cause confusion.

All sensational or sublime elements are banned—there are no steep flowerbeds, colorful, exotic shrubs, copper beeches, or blackthorn. Next to well-mown lawns are large expanses of high grass; alongside the grassy alleys grow conically, spirally, cylindrically trimmed hedges, interspersed with ancient statues and obelisks, to assert the idea of methodized nature cherished by many French philosophers of the Age of Enlightenment.

The park, created around a few pre-existing trees—metasequoias, lime trees—chestnuts, oaks, elms, taxodium, butternuts, and white poplars— has a trapezoidal shape, and is surrounded by a belt of tall trees that thicken in the four corners to create groves that spread on to a wide, elliptic meadow. The visitor can get an idea of this, thanks to the suggestive but limited glimpse allowed by a gate.

Further evidence of the stylistic influences of Paolo Genta Ternavasio, and perhaps one of the most important elements of a successful garden, is gradualness: the viewer's inability to grasp the whole immediately, the necessity of discovering it progressively, slowly. The gardens present a series of unexpected visual impressions, which are apt to create emotions, but are carefully controlled so as not to jeopardize the sense of reserve and total balance of this universe.

On the site of a sixteenth-century Franciscan monastery, a villa was built in the eighteenth century, consisting of two long wings intersecting at right angles.

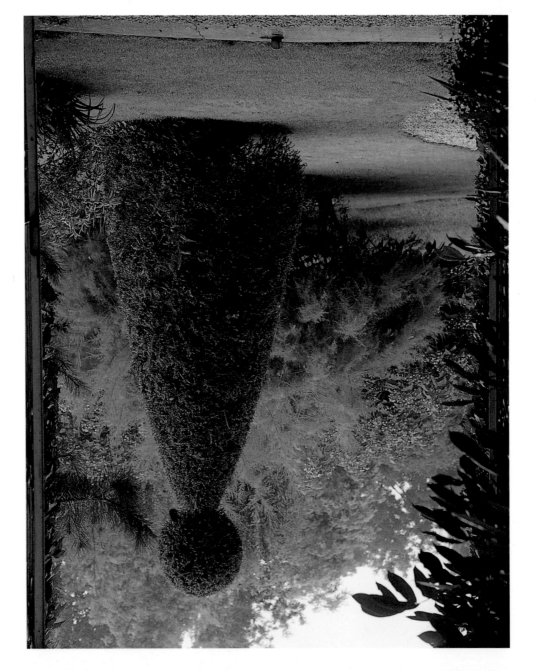

Above and opposite: Sophisticated,
geometric volumes of box trees, shaped
by topiary art, interrupt the early
romantic tone of the garden.

The garden's British inspiration is
filtered by a fundamental rationalism
of French origin.

Above: Among the brick paths, regular hedges, and obelisks, an enclosed garden is concealed behind a brick wall, a remnant of the former monastery.

Following pages: Views of the garden. The pagoda standing out against the water lily-covered lake is a quotation from the eighteenth-century Piedmontese taste for chinoiseries.

Ratti Garden
Como

During his fifty-year career, between 1931 and 1986, Pietro Porcinai constantly strove in his designs for a synchrony with nature, devoid of symbolic content but pervaded with mysticism. The gardens he designed in Tuscany are characterized by an austere geometry, measured forms, and a small number of select species, in a spirit that radically departs from the nineteenth-century tendency to collect the largest possible number of botanical varieties.

In other regions his design took a different course, noticeable in the Ratti park, with its panoramic view over Lake Como, on the road to Cernobbio. The huge villa, a refined interpretation of the classical architectural tradition, especially Palladian, was built after 1920 by Mino Fiocchi and transformed in 1953 by the architects Caccia Dominioni and Mongiardino. The 2.3 acre park stretches around the villa, up towards the hill, and in a gentle downward slope towards the swimming pool.

Covered by a green mantle of *Ampelopsis*, the house has practically lost its architectural features, becoming the center of the botanical webs that constitute the park. Lower down, there is another garden where, on an area of the same dimensions, three other villas serve as seat and offices for the Rattis' famous silk trade. The idea that presided over the conception of the park—on which both Porcinai and the owner, Antonio Ratti, collaborated about twenty-five years ago—was to give the azalea the leading part: there are over a thousand specimens including every possible variety. When they bloom, between April and June, they are the dominant color in the park, a color that slowly moves from pale yellow to white, pale pink to bright red, going through the complete palette of intermediate shades. Wide green lawns break up the plants' exuberance with a carpet of *agrostis* grass, sown piece by piece in a complicated and demanding process and, unlike the other types of grass, it requires continuous maintenance and must be entirely renewed after eight or ten years.

Hundreds of tall trees and low shrubs animate the park: cypresses, ilexes, plane trees, birches, pines, and various species of cedars, *Ficus repens*, and *Cotoneaster*. A host of Japanese dwarf maples add to the general score with their comforting horizontal growth. Wisteria, numerous varieties of camellias, nemesias, rhododendrons, and dozens of rose bushes in patches or geometric borders, combine their different colors in the variegated tapestry of villa Ratti's park. In the greenhouses, gardeners cultivate the plants that will replace the dead or seasonal ones, or look after the more fragile species.

"I have done everything in my life, except eat fire," said Pietro Porcinai, probably the most important figure in Italian contemporary landscape gardening. This garden is the result of his enthusiasm and unquenchable thirst for knowledge, together with the passion of manufacturer and patron Antonio Ratti, who is greatly involved in cultural matters—in December 1995, a textile center bearing his name was inaugurated at the Metropolitan Museum of Art in New York, and for ten years now, the Ratti Foundation has been promoting cultural, artistic, and technological initiatives and research. The Ratti gardens reflect the elegance of Porcinai's strict poetics, confronted with a local tradition characterized by the overflowing, eighteenth-century presence of colored patches of flowers.

Built by Mino Fiocchi in the twenties in imitation of the classical style, the villa disappears under the greenery of the creepers that cover it. The lawn is interrupted by a wide flowerbed of nemesia hybrids.

Above and opposite: The swimming pool is hemmed in by an ilex hedge, cotoneasters, azaleas, cypresses, maple trees, and a wall of Ficus repens.

Following pages: The garden is crossed by the stone paths typical of Pietro Porcinai's poetics.

The classical style of the garden's entire layout is emphasized in some suggestive spots. There is an enormous variety of arboreal species: birch trees, types of cedars, plane trees, and cotoneasters, cypresses, ilexes, and dwarf Japanese maple trees.

Trenzanesio Garden
Rodano (Milan)

Morning drizzles down onto the garden. . . . At the top of a muddy slope, near a cross turned green and black by dampness, a wooden worm-eaten door is set into the derelict enclosure. . . . At the bottom, the ruins of the cloister with the ivy and the dried flowers, and in the cracks of the fallen stones, some yellow flowers full of rainwater. . . . Thick veils of cobwebs. . . . the stone bench is overgrown with moss. . . . You can hear the steady dripping. . . . of the water that mourns the sadness of the dead garden.

Take the poignant feeling of melancholy and neglect produced by the *jardin muerto*, from Federico Garcia Lorca's *Impressiones y Paisajes* (Impression and Landscapes), add the attraction exerted by unknown worlds to which youthful imaginations give a special appeal, and you have the clue to the true resurrection of the Trenzanesio park.

Every day at dawn, when the present owner was still a boy, he would walk past the magic white shape of the villa; this is how he started nursing the dream that finally became true in 1955. That year marks the incredible rebirth of a plot of unspoiled nature, annexed to a garden designed in the sophisticated baroque style, located only five miles from the center of Milan. Motorists driving along the *Rivoltana*, a few steps from Linate airport, may well be astonished at the sight of the deer running among the trees.

The estate spreads over one thousand acres, of which five hundred twenty-five are tilled agricultural land (the former hunting/shooting grounds), and the remaining four hundred seventy-five constitute the park proper. Far from the majestic wrought-iron entry gates, at the end of a long drive lined with poplars, the original villa was built as a summer residence in 1560 by Cardinal Giulio Litta, archbishop of Milan.

The style of the villa shows some schematized characteristics of the Palladian style. In fact, Giovanni da Pedemuro, who was responsible for the project, had worked as an apprentice stone cutter in Andrea Palladio's Vicenza workshop. Strongly influenced by Michele Sanmicheli, Pedemuro was responsible, together with Giovanni Pittoni, for a good number of the "modern style" sculptures and funeral monuments in Vicenza in the first half of the sixteenth century. With Palladio, Pedemuro presented in 1546 the project for the Vicenza Basilica, the great loggia built around the gothic meeting-hall of the Council of the Five Hundred.

The villa remained in the hands of the Marquesses Litta until 1800; then, when Barbara married Count Greppi, it became part of the latter's possessions. The estate began to decline in the middle of the nineteenth century: land was sold, and the house, after becoming a textile factory, fell into total neglect and decay at the end of World War II. It took the two architects Tommaso Buzzi and Alberto Menin eight years to restore the villa's ancient magnificence. Little by little the original estate was reconstituted, as field after field was bought back.

One day, a 1630 engraving was found by the greatest of luck: it described in a profusion of detail the early-baroque garden that Litta wanted. Because of this find, the park came back to life: twenty thousand specimens were planted, fountains and obelisks were erected, and statues and ancient architectural elements, mainly of Venetian origin, were bought by the dozen. Cranes, peacocks, two thousand deer, black and white swans, brightly-colored parrots populated the spaces of the formal garden and the "wild" sections of the park. In the canals, the trout flashed to and fro and the somnolent carps flourished, having for centuries inhabited the ditches of the gentry's *horti*. As if filtered through the romantic requirements of the English landscape garden, the baroque idiom adopts the usual geometrical box forms, softened by topiaries and the sculptures and waterworks. The Po valley countryside penetrates and enlarges the guarded geometry of the garden. At Trenzanesio, the linear itineraries and the delicate balance between the fancifully trimmed hedges, the parterres, and the airy views display a typically British attention to a blend of natural elements and the art of making the best use of what one has at hand, a precept deeply rooted in the Lombard culture.

The tenacity of the family has saved the estate from a project for the widening of a railway line. Now, this most improbable refuge in the modern, contaminated context of the Milan suburbs has been classified among protected areas, and is destined to become the seat of a prestigious scientific foundation.

Villa Trenzanesio was built by Giovanni da Pedemuro, Andrea Palladio's collaborator, for Cardinal Giulio Litta, archbishop of Milan. Its rigorous architectural style shows a Palladian stamp.

The rigorous topiary art is softened by a discreet touch, and the greenery is enlivened by dozens of ancient statues.

Today the park is the seat of an important scientific foundation.

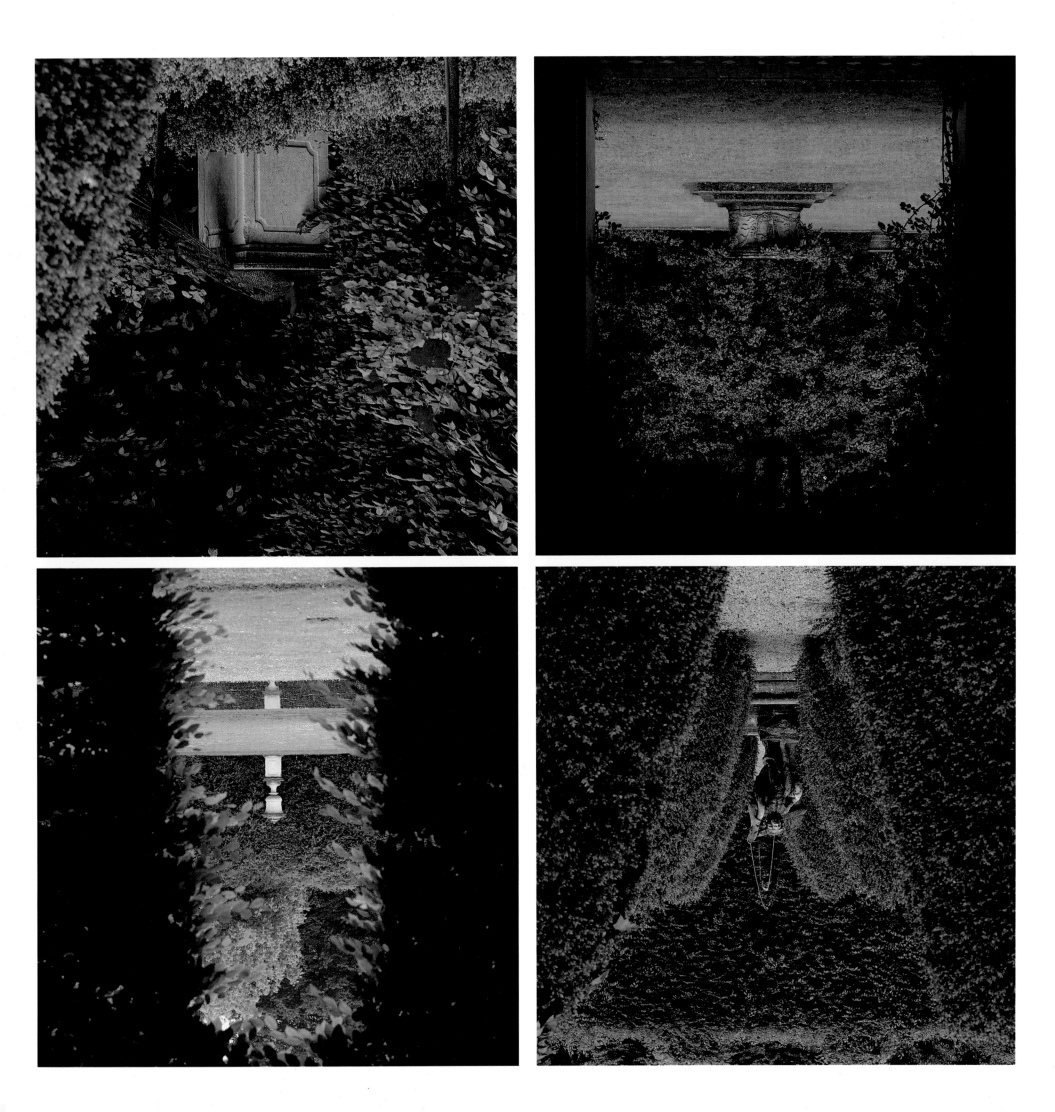

Previous pages: Comparable to the layout of the Italian garden of Villa Gamberaia, the formal parterre is connected to the Paduan countryside by the vista composed of rows of black poplars.

Above and opposite: The baroque reinvention of spaces is blended with a romantic note of nineteenth-century English inspiration.

Villa Rizzardi
Negrar di Valpolicella (Verona)

On entering I also see / A vast scenery of foliage. / The incredulous eye lingers there for a while. / Then follows the wide alley running in the middle of / A double row of a hundred white / Marble statues and a hundred green cedars . . .

The verses that Abbot Saverio Bettinelli dedicated to the owner of the now-disappeared Villa Corner al Paradiso, near Castelfranco Veneto, perfectly evoke the majestic green prospects of Villa Rizzardi at Negrar.

In the Veneto, rather than existing as a self-sufficient work of art, the garden becomes an aesthetic ornament of the landscape, contributing a certain quality to the surrounding land. Built at the end of the eighteenth century and transformed in the second half of the nineteenth, Villa Rizzardi stands amidst the famous Valpolicella vineyards, a few miles from Verona.

The villa was built for Count Antonio Rizzardi, a wealthy, cosmopolitan man, who had spent many years traveling for business in faraway countries. The villa reflects its owner's tastes, matured in heterogeneous cultural environments. The count's wife, an Englishwoman, probably played a decisive part as upholder of the new theories on the art of gardening, a theme then at the heart of intellectual debates in Great Britain.

Created in 1783 and designed by Luigi Trezza (whose drawings can be seen at the Verona Municipal Library, and who also contributed to the remodeling of the Giusti's urban garden), the park is built on three levels, linked together by an alley edged with cypresses that frame the surrounding landscape. Considered one of the last authentic formal parks, visibly modeled according to the Italian tradition of scenic spatial design, the garden is delineated by vegetal walls and the geometric traces of box hedges, disseminated on the parterre gravel with a sober graphic taste that seems inspired by French seventeenth- or eighteenth-century examples. The colorful flowerbeds and the theatrical terraces and central alley leading from the villa to the theater are clearly in the Italian tradition, as is the belvedere, which provides a privileged point of view on the surrounding rural countryside, where the vineyards and fruit trees become ornamental, just like the statues and hedges of the park. On the other hand, a British tone is provided by the wood, by a certain taste for the picturesque that breaks the background pattern of the hedges, and by some exotic varieties of trees of Chinese, Japanese, or Indian origin.

The secret garden is dug into the hill slope next to the house, and can be reached directly from the second floor, across a small bridge. A small waterfall gushing out among the fragrant greenness of the plants brings to mind paintings by Hubert Robert, as if to corroborate the old link between gardening and landscape painting.

The park is reached from the top, down the various terraces of the hill. After the parterre, marked off by box hedges with a circular basin in the center, on the second level the green mantle opens up onto the lemon garden. This circular space is surrounded with large terra-cotta pots for the plants. In winter they used to be kept in the lemon-house, which is now turned into a tea-house. Finally, on the axis leading towards the villa, the spectacular hornbeam gallery appears—a typical, famous element of the Venetian rural gentry's landscape. In this case, the trees have been shaped into a curve, the top of which is open to let in the sunlight.

The alley leads to a niche surrounded by four splendid cypresses. More cypresses, tall and majestic, with a *Yucca constricta* lost in their midst, lead to the entrance of the open-air theater, guarded by two stone lions. Created in 1796, when the rest of the park was already finished, it is the biggest Italian open-air theater of its type. Dug into the hill, it is enclosed by a vegetal wall indented with niches that half-conceal statues. The cavea is woven in the clear geometry of the box hedges arranged in neo-classic order, only interrupted and set off by the rough stone steps that give access. Without clashing with the theater's airy, rational space, the cypress alley resumes the path to the belvedere, an octagonal stone structure framed by a balustrade decorated with jocund putti, divided in two by a central stairway, and commanding a spectacular panoramic view of the Valpolicella vineyards.

The wood was originally composed of oak trees only, but is today interspersed with various species, mostly elms. Among the shady trees under which crouch mysterious stone animals, there is yet another invention concealed in the park: the circular folie, an open-air room built in a period when picturesque ruins were fashionable, and whose niches carved in the tuff walls and decorated with sheaves and elegant stone frames enclose mythological divinities.

This is a park that, in its various levels, becomes a landscape of many superimposed gardens, a sum of different languages united by their one natural context.

Situated among the famous Valpolicella vineyards, not far from Verona, the villa was built in the second half of the eighteenth century by Count Antonio Rizzardi. The garden was created in 1783, designed by Luigi Trezza, who also worked for the Giustis in Verona, and at Villa Brenzone of Punta San Vigilio.

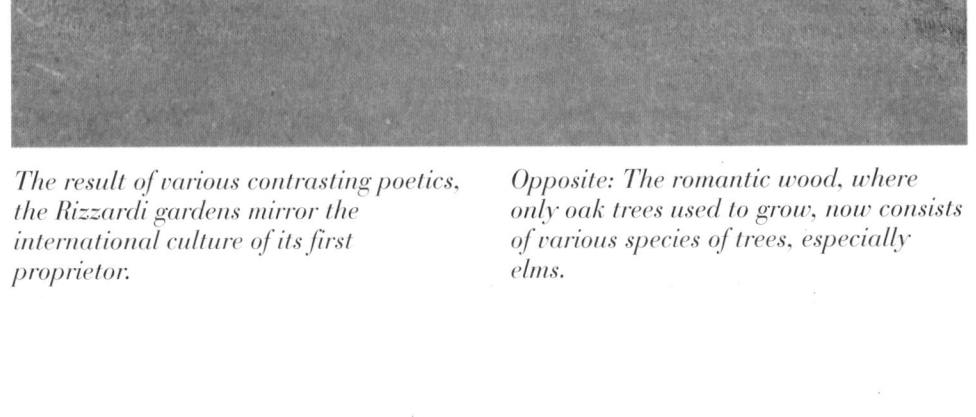

The result of various contrasting poetics, the Rizzardi gardens mirror the international culture of its first proprietor.

Opposite: The romantic wood, where only oak trees used to grow, now consists of various species of trees, especially elms.

The largest of its type in Italy, the amphitheater has been dug into the rocky hill. It is enclosed by a vegetal wall with niches inhabited by statues. Bottom: Built on three levels linked together by a cypress alley, the park is entered from the top.

A creation of the later eighteenth-century picturesque, an open-air chamber houses mythological divinities, in the niches carved out of the tuff walls. Bottom: Crowned by a balustrade supporting jocund putti, the octagonal belvedere provides an aristocratic viewpoint on the surrounding countryside.

Giusti del Giardino Gardens
Verona

Yesterday evening . . . in the Giusti gardens . . . I had the honor of walking for the first time under the pine trees, of watching this noble, melancholy tree rise against the blue sky. The garden climbs upwards on the rock, as if there were an infinity of gardens one on top of the other, until a very wide, splendid view opens up in front of your eyes. The whole of Verona lies at your feet, with on the left the pretty plain that stretches as far as Venice, and on the right, in the distance, the blue mountains, under a unique sky, the like of which does not exist.

Thus wrote Johann Gottfried Herder to his wife Carolina in September 1788, so distracted by the beauty of the park that he mistook its majestic cypresses for pines.

The city of Verona is woven with sophisticated gothic signs, combined with the echoes of Roman civilization—summed up by the massive structure of the arena—and the city's history intertwines with that of the Giusti family.

At the beginning of the eighteenth century, justly proud of their garden—an emblem of family power celebrated for its beauty—the Giusti di Santa Maria in Organo family added the predicate *del Giardino* (of the garden) to their name. The garden was begun in 1570 by Agostino Giusti and is a fair representation of its creator's sophistication and culture. A Venetian patrician and gentleman of the grand duke of Tuscany (from which region the family had emigrated to Ghibelline Verona at the beginning of the fourteenth century), he was a refined patron who was both a keen collector and music lover.

As if to underline Giusti's connection with two such different milieus—the Venetian, exemplified by its functional garden poetics, devoid of any metaphysical tricks; and the Tuscan, devoted to the most daring talent and allegorical transfiguration—the park combines instances of late humanism with the affected and genial complexity of sixteenth-century mannerism. Cut in two by the geometric austerity of the cypress alley, the flat zone is subdivided into quadrangular areas by secondary, perpendicular alleys.

In the past, a background of tall cypresses outlined cabinets where statues and fountains stood out against the lines of the box hedges. In the eighteenth century, Luigi Trezza (who also worked at Villa Brenzone and at Rizzardi Gardens of Negrar) transformed the perspective view, cutting down the tall trees and weaving the parterres with flowerbeds in the French manner, each embellished by Lorenzo Muttoni's statues. The vast collection of Roman epigraphs are a reminder of Agostino Giusti's refined literary tastes, representative of an aristocracy strongly learned in classical culture.

Among the green crags leading up to Mount San Zeno, however, in spite of the serene broken tympanum that frames it, the entrance to the grotto proclaims the failure of Renaissance reason, as though it had exploded to be left to the mercy of Dionysian forces. Pervaded with mysterious symbolism, the cave becomes a microcosmic manifestation of the four elements. The air, the water, and the fire historically hide in the cave, dug into the dark womb of the earth—the first in the guise of alpine flowers, the second represented by shells and mother-of-pearl, and the fire alluded to with red coral. The ordinary or anamorphic mirrors, the gurgling of the water spurting out of the urn supported by a faun, the play of echoes and vocal distortions, everything is meant to increase the pathos of the place, an arena where the "durable" competes with Time, marked by the pulsations of the fountain. The labyrinth, redefined in the eighteenth century by architect Luigi Trezza, prolongs *en plein air* the tricks and vertigoes of an increasingly impenetrable and less reassuring nature.

A nineteenth-century transformation into a romantic park was somewhat reverted in 1930s, but only recently has the Giustis' passion for their park—shared and supported by the architect Pier Fausto Bagatti Valsecchi—driven them to undertake a restoration based on thorough historical and iconographic research.

A compulsory halting place for German intellectuals traveling towards Rome, the gardens were begun in 1570 by Agostino Giusti, a humanist and patron. At the beginning of the eighteenth century, the great fame of the gardens and the prestige that accompanies them induced the Santa Maria in Organo branch of the Giusti family to adopt the predicate del Giardino.

Opposite: The classical statues, the reassuring outlines of the late Renaissance portal tympanum, and the vast collection of Roman epigraphs testify that the client belonged to humanistic circles.

The box hedges were once hemmed-in by proper cypress walls that shaped open-air chambers. In the eighteenth century, the architect Luigi Trezza had them cut down to aerate the garden.

The grotto and the large Bomarzo-style mask indicate the introduction of the sophistications of Central Italian mannerism into the orderly Venetian context of late Renaissance gardens. Opposite: In the secluded parts of the garden, nature seems absorbed in itself and its obscure forces, in the best early romantic tradition.

Villa Emo Capodilista alla Montecchia
Selvazzano Dentro (Padua)

Among the hills that surround the city of Padua, in a landscape that has kept its particular well-balanced beauty despite the transformations of the last decades, rises Villa Emo Capodilista alla Montecchia. Built on top of a low hill, reached along a slow-climbing road shaded by lime trees, the villa is delineated by a copse of oak trees, a dam on the well-ordered rows of vineyards. Past a small circular planting is the summit of the hill, a flat, clover-shaped terrace confined by high retaining walls. The impression of feudal lordship over the surrounding territory (once dominated by a medieval castle on the very spot where the present villa stands) is confirmed by the flights of stairs that, from each of the four sides, lead to up the villa gates, guarded by eighteenth- century statues.

Characterized on each façade by airy loggias animated by five arcades, the building is hemmed in by four sturdy turrets, another reminder of the Venetian neo-feudalism of the end of the sixteenth century. And the strange crenelation that decorates the top gives Villa Emo a touch of the fantastic. The villa was built by Dario Varotari, a sixteenth-century Paduan painter and architect, and a delicate creator of formal gardens. Since the villa was meant for the pleasures of shooting and aristocratic banqueting, it has no real residential or agricultural functions. The open sections of the architecture predominate over the closed—from the inside it seems as if the structure was conceived to frame parts of the outside scenery. With its trees and lush fields, the Venetian countryside bursts into the house in an endless vista of landscape fragments. And while this landscape, seen from the arcades and set between the mannerist, grotesque paintings of the vaults, takes on a quality of pictorial narration in the villa's rooms, the "unreal" architectural stamp of its exterior prospects makes the villa appear from the outside as an imaginary background taken from Paolo Veronese's ornamental frescoes.

Woven with multicolored flowerbeds alternating with innumerous shades of roses, the garden is outlined by the dwarf privet hedges. More rustic and rarer than the usual dark, shiny mantle of box trees, the privet adds a touch of ancestral fragrance to the formal mannerist requirements, and conjures up the atmosphere of walled-in kitchen gardens.

Sovereign of the cultivated fields that surround it, the villa is connected to this rustic dimension by the groups of Italian pine trees growing in the corners of the garden. Carved in Custoza stone, the statues in the garden represent couples of young lovers, and lend the inevitable note of eighteenth-century Arcadia, present in every Venetian aristocratic context. The last link with the countryside landscape, four little bridges with an aura of the Middle Ages allow a panoramic walk along the garden perimeter.

Thanks to the dedication of its owners, particularly Count Giordano Emo Capodilista, responsible for the management of the estate, la Montecchia has retained the charms of its original beauty.

Situated on a small eminence among the hills that encircle the city of Padua, Villa Emo Capodilista dominates the countryside of vineyards and cultivated fields in which it is set. Built at the end of the sixteenth century by Dario Varotari, father of the famous Padovanino, it is characterized by its airy loggias, which predominate over the "solid" spaces, and its odd architectural features that give it a theatrical appearance.
Following pages: The elegant Italian hanging garden is laid out in front of the building, accentuating the slope of the hill, and is enclosed in a rocky, clover-shaped terrace. Rather than being made of box, the hedges are the rarer and more rustic dwarf privet.

Barbarigo Gardens
Valsanzibio (Padua)

All the sites lying northwards are wretched, like Valsancibio, Garrignano, Toreggia, Luvigiano, Abano, Praglia and others. And although there are sites with beautiful views . . . the fact that the eye is immediately arrested by a marsh produces a strange impression, and it explains the wretchedness of the Euganei hills which, more than often, have their crown lost in thick fogs and their heels drowned in the marshes or swamps; and just as a host of clouds can be seen wandering over their crests, so endless reeds can be seen to undulate at their feet . . .

In this diatribe written at the beginning of the seventeenth century, Scipione Mercuri, a doctor from Monselice, bluntly denies the salubrity of the Euganei hills. This region was already famous for the villas that had been built there, beginning with the sophisticated Renaissance residence of the Paduan bishops built in 1529 by Falconetto (or Cornaro) at Luvigliano. Mercuri's warning certainly did not prevent Procurator Antonio Barbarigo's intervention on a family estate, and he turned it into one of the most remarkable eighteenth-century gardens of the Veneto. Brother of Gregorio and son of Gianfrancesco Barbarigo, who bought the estate from the Contarinis in 1627 and increased it by purchasing other strips of land before 1650, Antonio also inherited the house which his father had built there. This house was mentioned by Andrea Piccolomini, an astronomer who, contradicting Mercuri, praised the most perfect air and the various conveniences the house offered all day long. Apart from a few ornamental elements, the "rabbit warren" built in 1693, and later additions on the master's house (1694), most of the construction occurred between June 1, 1665 (when the contract for the pillars for the front gates was signed) and January 22, 1670 (when the surveyor Nicolò Ratti was summoned to appraise the works carried out at Valsanzibio).

Although it emphasizes the representation of the residential building, a painting dating from the end of the seventeenth century (Procurator Barbarigo died in 1702) clearly demonstrates the projected design—the neat, geometric meter of the garden spaces, outlined by two symmetrical alleys, rectilinear, extremely long, and edged with trees. The fountains, the fish ponds, the watercourse that winds it way towards the lake, dominated by the stagy perspective point of Diana's Bath, all proclaim the water's central power as the life force of the whole garden. (Together with Aeolus, to whom the temple and the rocky hillock are dedicated, Diana was the goddess who presided over the natural realm, rural and hunting activities.) Splinters from the baroque universe, the folies (the "rabbit warren" and the splendid box labyrinth) introduce the play of deceit and hedonistic amusement.

Although he was at the center of Venetian political life and had held important offices, reaching the rank of Procurator, Antonio Barbarigo excluded any self-glorification or reference to his public career from his gardens. He probably conceived by himself the complicated iconographic program, and by means of numerous inscriptions and allegories, he seems to confirm the perfect serenity of this rural oasis, compared to the artificial, inconclusive chaos of political struggle. Like Horace, who praised the simple comforts of his villa in Sabina, Antonio proclaims his ideals in a sophisticated play of contrasts and metaphors. In the end, idleness and peace are the purpose of movement. If the beauties of the garden are all of nature and none of Art—a concept that owes much to the Venetian tradition although here it seems to stray from the antimetaphysical local tradition—the fact that the troubles of urban life are excluded from this enchanted enclosure, where the Graces reign, where pleasure rules, enables it to be the seat of laughter, not a place for tears.

However, the real symbolism of the statues and waterworks, architectures and microcosmic elements may be more alarming and mysterious. From the Spain of the *Siglo de Oro*, Calderon warns us that "the whole sky is an omen, and the whole world is a wonder." Here at Valsanzibio, Chronos, bearing on his back a heavy polyhedron (he is almost crushed under its weight!) quotes the words *volan col tempo l'hore e fuggon gli anni* (the hours fly with time and the years flee). Is the baroque iconographer referring to the serene time of the seasons' cyclic return, or is he alluding to the transient implacability of the passing years? Or does he intend to stigmatize the ephemeral graces of a park as an illusory and ludicrous rampart created by Art against the inescapable, Dionysiac passing of things?

A culture like the baroque is difficult to decipher, for it absolutely presupposes that the game is without rules. And with the inscription *Quivi è l'inferno, quivi il paradiso* (Here is hell, here is the paradise) proclaiming its labyrinthine contradictions, Valsanzibio is a complete, faithful representation of the Baroque.

Inherited by the Michiels, the villa later belonged to the Martinengos, who "landscaped" part of the garden at the beginning of the nineteenth century. After belonging to the Donà dalle Rose family, it is at present owned by Counts Pizzoni-Ardemani, who devote immense care to keeping it in good condition.

A simple building erected by Antonio Barbarigo in the 1660s, today the villa belongs to Counts Pizzoni Ardemani.

Opposite: A view of the garden, in which the strict box hedges are interspersed with wider spaces featuring statues and fountains. The entire layout of the Valsanzibio garden is characterized by the presence of water.

An apparent evocation of the theatrical architectures of the baroque age, Diana's Bath is a kind of triumphal gate of great dramatic impact.

Opposite: Mythological baroque statues punctuate the greenery of the trees and box hedges.

The labyrinth is a splendid geometrical structure, and an unavoidable complement of the baroque garden.

Opposite: The fountains dedicated to the rivers and winds, seen from the top of Diana's Bath, which frames the vista of this garden axis.

Villa Emo Capodilista
La Rivella-Monselice (Padua)

. . . you have to travel across the English countryside to understand what the banks of the Brenta must have looked like a few centuries ago, when, as Andrea Palladio wrote, tired of the city's turmoil, the soul could find there "great refreshment and comfort." . . . At Rivella di Monselice, with the magic wand of her unerring taste, Giuseppina Emo Capodilista has given a new life to a small Palladian jewel, and you remain astonished when you realize that two years ago it was but a damaged shell, reduced to being a granary.

This is what Mario Praz wrote in 1967, as he melancholically pored over the modern environmental decay of the Venetian countryside, a landscape of peaceful, Arcadian serenity, which the aristocracy of the past had dotted with beautiful villas, "in order to retire from the hubbub of the rabble."

The salvaging of Villa Emo alla Rivella is indeed remarkable. An elegant, austere example of sixteenth-century architecture attributed to Vincenzo Scamozzi, it clearly speaks the language of neo-feudalism with its compact, severe volumes, and its abstract design. This architectural idiom announces the end of the stylistic harmony between aristocratic existence and the surrounding agricultural landscape during a time when the enlightened lord was directly involved in the cultivation of his fields. Now, the villas grew more and more numerous. They no longer fit the agrarian functionality, but became real and proper sanctuaries for the gentry, increasingly sumptuous when built by the more recent aristocracy.

The villa was finished in 1588 for the noble Contarini family, and after fluctuating fortunes over the course of the years, became the property of the Emo Capodilistas; at present, Marina Emo resides there. In 1892, when Monsignor Andrea Maldura made Angelo Emo his heir, villa and gardens were in a state of complete neglect. It was only in 1966 that the present owner's parents began restoring them. They started with the inside of the villa, embellishing the drawing-rooms of the first floor with mannerist frescoes by Battista Del Moro, found in a ruined villa in the province of Verona. In order to animate its discreet, classical rigor, Count and Countess Emo decided to insert elements of space, color, and romantic spontaneity into the original design of the sixteenth-century park. Drawn by box hedges on the small parterre in front of the villa, their initials testify to this new intervention.

Variety mainly springs from the multicolored intrusion of the flowers. Inhabited by numerous carps, two seventeenth-century fish ponds are bordered with vast flowerbeds planted with roses, bearing regal or poetical names that sometimes hint at the delicate shades of the flower, such as the white 'Iceberg', and the pink 'Queen Elizabeth' and 'Mona Lisa'. An enormous bush of the famous 'Paul Neyron' variety, created in 1869 by Paul Levet in Lyons, produces big pink flowers streaked with lilac; their shade is so unique and original that it creates an altogether new color. Between May and June, the well-ordered, symmetrical decorum of the parterres is animated by the variegated surprises of callas, irises, nymphaea, hyacinths, and white water lilies.

At the back of the villa, nature gets the upper hand again, and the garden merges progressively into the Venetian landscape that encloses it. A long, shady alley of hornbeams, almost a replica of the one in Veronese's frescoes at Maser, offers its protection to the various snowdrops, *Scilla bifolia*, primroses, *Hepatica nobilis*, *Pulmonaria officinalis*, hellebores, meadow-saffrons, *Corydalis cava*, and wood-anemonies. Delineated by the hornbeam copse, the airy central parterre is edged with two long mixed borders, experimentation laboratories for the owner's fantasies, blooming continuously from March to October. More secret and romantic, a walk along an alley of magnolias leads to a watercourse that widens into a small lake. Wide patches of gaudy, fawn-colored *Hemerocallis* and flowering pomegranates serve as a counterpoint to the measured rhythm of the magnolias. On the left, a long canal is underlined by a host of creamy white oriental irises. In the thicket, the pale green nuance of the slender bamboo canes and willows combines with colors that illuminate this secluded, secret spot.

There are innumerable surprises kept by this park, a blend of sixteenth-century style and romantic fancy, hidden from the Padua-Battaglia Terme road by a thick mantle of poplars.

Attributed to the architect Vincenzo Scamozzi and built in 1588 for the Contarini family, the polished sixteenth-century volumes of Villa Emo alla Rivella stand out above the formal parterres that lie in front.

Outlined by the symmetrical lines of the hedges, the mixed borders—a Gertrude Jekyll touch in a Venetian context—act as a laboratory for the owner's botanical experiments.

Opposite: A view of the sinuous lines of the sixteenth-century-type parterre in front of the villa.

Above and opposite: Another feature of Villa Emo Capodilista is the roses: the white 'Iceberg' and 'Mona Lisa', 'Queen Elizabeth' and the splendid iride corollas of 'Paul Neyron', pink streaked with lilac, created in Lyon by Paul Levet in 1869. The flowerbeds are enlivened by irises, daisies, and roses in a harmonious combination of colors. The tall wall of poplars defends the garden from any foreign intrusion, and especially the motor traffic that flows close to this protected area.

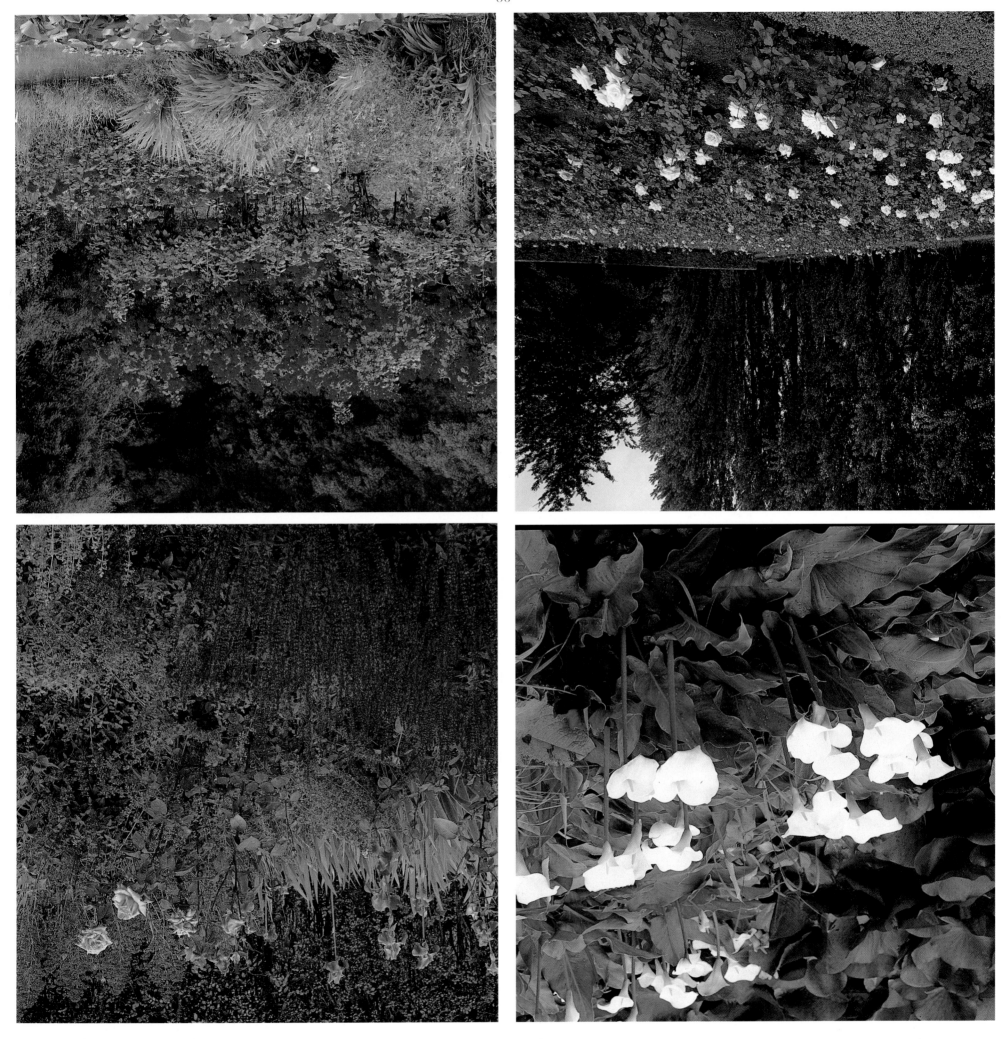

Meli-Lupi di Soragna Gardens
Soragna (Parma)

Lost among poplars and elm trees, in the opulent greenness of the Emilian plain, for a thousand years the Soragna fortress has lorded over the fertile landscape near Fidenza, the former Borgo San Donnino. The austere, bulky manor, familiarly surrounded by its village, bears evidence to the feudal pomp and many-centuried history of the Lupis' power (later Meli-Lupis). Whereas the exterior of the fortress is characterized by a vigorous and severe compactness, the inside is a triumphant explosion of baroque ornamental exuberance. In the sumptuous State Hall, the Donne Forti Hall, the Nuptial Bedchamber, the Gallery (dedicated to the glory of the poets, from Pindar and Anacreon to Dante, Petrarch, and Tasso), everywhere, magnificent pieces of furniture, tapestries, and ornamental objects refined by centuries of aristocratic everyday life, decorate the rooms of the castle, now partially open to the public. The present owners, Princess Violetta and her son Diophoebus, live in the private wing, and although they have conceded access to the ancient walls, they keep absolute dominion over the gardens, and visitors only get partial glimpses of them, as they are framed through the windows of the fortress.

The golden days of Soragna Park date back to 1703, when Admiral Marquess Giuseppe Meli-Lupi, influenced by a Venetian culture in which the theme of the garden was central, undertook some important transformations. Just behind the walls, a vast basin was dug; filled with water, it became a small, picturesque lake, surrounded by greenery. In a context of Arcadian graces, an island was indispensable, and it was not dedicated to the Cytherean seductions of Aphrodite, but to Mercury, whose bust stands out on the side of the lake. For over two hundred years, this messenger of the Olympian gods and protector of merchants and thieves alike has been meditating between the Pillars of Hercules, the extreme limit of the world that can be known by human beings. The small troupe of mythological statues is the work of unknown Venetian artists, commissioned by Marquess Giuseppe who had been charmed by the beauties of the Brenta villas, this Parnassus of the declining Serene Republic's last earthly splendors.

Among the wide clearings guarded by ancient trees (including a hickory measuring over sixteen feet in diameter), in natural surroundings that once more seem to spring directly from sixteenth-century Venetian landscape painting, gods, nymphs, and allegorical representations weave patterns, perhaps in an effort to indicate cognitive routes. The grotto, now blocked by an internal landslide, is guarded by Mars. A memory of the Admiral's perilous voyages, the small lake becomes an invitation to discover the unknown, to run the risks of one's destiny, whatever it may be. The uncommonly suggestive power of Soragna Park would undoubtedly have been appreciated by a refined French traveler at the end of the eighteenth century—President Charles Dupaty. Disparaging gardens that are "commissioned by pride, symmetrical, monotonous," he praises those in which "the knowledge of and love for nature's beauties charm the eye, the imagination, and the heart, suggesting ever-new fancies." Soragna is by rights one of these gardens.

The open basin of the small lake, and the fort, which is crowned by Ghibelline merlons. The terrace concludes the two-hundred-foot-long Poets' Gallery, which develops independently of the quadrangular volumes of the fortress.

Admiral Giuseppe Meli Lupi, Marquess of Soragna, had the mythological sculptures placed in the park at the beginning of the eighteenth century. Among the low *hillocks that surround the fortress, the statues punctuate a sort of ideal itinerary through the greenery.*

Guarded by its watchtowers, the terrace
evokes the great feudal past of the Meli
Lupis of Soragna.

Opposite: Arcadian suggestions of light
and shade, of the green trees mirrored in
the waters of the small lake, confronted
with the gothic stamp of the big ogival
arch of the open basin.

Watermill Garden
Val Bure (Pistoia)

"In her, a pretty disarray is an effect of Art . . ."

This verse from Boileau seems most appropriate to depict the picturesque charm of the garden created by Paolo Ignesti around a eight-century-old watermill near Pistoia. Far from disrupting the spontaneous harmony of the place, Ignesti has complied with the undulating morphology of the ground and the pre-existing botanical species.

The garden is reached from the top and spreads out on three different levels. The visitor immediately enters a Mediterranean maquis, where the green of old olive trees with contorted trunks combines with the dark, shining green of the fragrant laurels. Roses climb against a thirteenth-century stone wall, and their scent rises above a background of sage and rosemary.

On the second terrace, the hydrangeas, ranging from bright pink to periwinkle blue and white, and the rhododendrons, with the golden yellow of the forsythia as a counterpoint, are accompanied by the constant movement of the waters that once supplied the mill. Impressions of shape, fragrance, and color, combinations and contrasts seem borrowed from Monet's paintings.

On the last terrace, the creator's respectful intervention become more obvious. There, Ignesti has given in to his fancy, with more daring, almost heretical associations, varying the pictorial theme, mixing the jasmin and the shy cyclamens with the sumptuous glow of the bougainvillea and the orchids. Shaded by wisteria, an ancient mule-track winds its way through blossoming shrubs and chestnut trees, towards the stone-roofed hut that conceals the greenhouses. The eccentric presence of the peacocks, with their bright, variegated feathers, brings life to this scenery, where the mainly impressionistic evocations blend with the rustic substance of the place.

In this garden, the creator's presence is light, discreet, as recommended in the eighteenth century by Marquess of Girardin in his *De la composition des paysages* (On the Composition of Gardens): "Without intruding anywhere, Art has perfectly seconded Nature . . ."

The tireless ampelopsis creeps up the walls of the ancient water mill. The waters of the stream that used to supply the mill trickle through the thick vegetation.
Following pages: a view of the garden with chestnut trees.

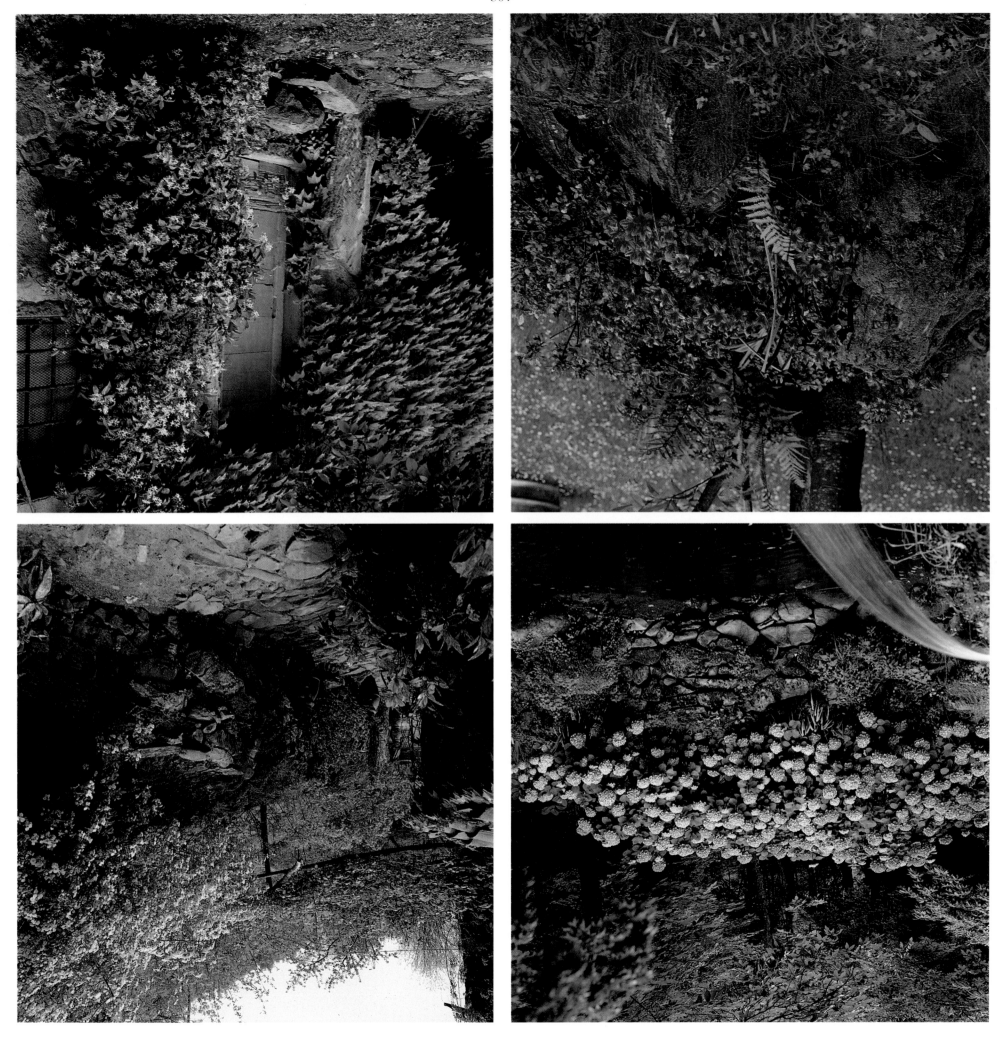

Previous pages: Impressionistic views are
composed by the wisteria's delicate
mauve, the hydrangea's various shades,
and the jasmin's discreet but fragrant
presence.

Above and opposite: The watercourse
unravels across the garden, like the mule
track which, shaded by ancient chestnut
trees, leads to the huts that conceal
the greenhouses.

Villa Garzoni
Collodi (Pistoia)

Under a thousand disguises the pretty cypress now joking, now serious, twists and stretches up. Now it is a tower, now a vessel, now it takes the semblance of a wild beast, now of a bird.

Francesco Sbarra's famous celebration poem *Le Pompe di Collodi*, was published in 1652, scrupulously describing the beauties of the garden ordered by Romano Garzoni, a member of the wealthy aristocracy of the baroque city of Lucca.

The park is documented as early as 1500 and, as represented in a 1633 drawing, it occupies a rather small area (154 yards by 220 yards), and is not in line with the villa but on its side. Enormous excavation works have remodeled the uneven profile of the hill where the villa is located into a geometric succession of terraces. Most uncommon, and created in the truly eighteenth-century conception of *maraviglia* and *movimento* (at that time, Motin, a French poet, asserted that "the soul of the whole world is but movement"), the strongly vertical orientation of the garden generates from the bottom a strange illusory effect, denying the wide breadth of the terraces. The terraces can only be perceived from the top, when they seem to assemble into a single soft slope, a tapestry of greens and bright colors.

The first phase of the garden's construction ended with the completion of the entrance parterres, at the time paved with a variegated texture of mannerist inspiration. At the same time, the labyrinth was taking shape, hidden in a small dell between the residential building and the declivity of the terraces. In the baroque period the labyrinth expresses the anxiety of a deeply shaken society. The confrontation between the green of the box trees and the colors of the flowers that embroider the first parterres in well ordered rows or eccentric volutes is another authentic feature of baroque culture.

In 1692, when the villa was already quite famous thanks to high-ranking visitors such as Anna de' Medici and Ferdinand of Hapsburg, the fountains finally appeared, and it is said that the garden was completely walled in. Most remarkable among its various components were:

. . . tall hedges of laurels and cypresses embellished by large windows, and balls made of the same cypresses . . . stairs of sandstone, walls covered with hedges of citrus fruits, with niches for statues and grottoes for small size waters and fountains, numerous sections of small myrtles, with figures of birds and others, and the vegetable garden, and fruit trees divided by hedges of roses, and on the flat space, a lawn with a most beautiful theater with hedges of cypresses and double alleys.

Everything seems more or less as it is nowadays. The semi-circular access area is decorated with two wide, circular basins, from which rises a single jet of water; the Garzoni coat-of-arms marks the tripartition of the first terrace. The garden is crossed transversally by three alleys: the Palm tree, the Emperors', and the Turk's alley. The link between the parts of the complex scenery is provided by the water stairs, guarded by two gigantic allegorical statues, one representing the Tuscan Pescia (river), accompanied by a lion, and the other, the Lucca Pescia, with a panther.

The grottoes (among which is Neptune's, paved with mosaics and inlaid with tuff), the spectacular stairways peopled by mocking terra-cotta monkeys, the theater, the graceful eighteenth-century bathhouse, as light as one of Mozart's sonatas, the exotic touch provided by the bamboo forest (planted later)—everything finds its conclusion at the basin that occupies the top part of the garden. The imposing representation of Fame, energetically blowing her bugle from which water gushes, dominates a mixed scene of *rocailles* and fantastic architectural elements, inlaid with stones, animated by volutes, eccentric urns, and the picturesque play of the small cascades that fall into the basin, on the surface of which float water lilies.

The location of the numerous terra-cotta and stone figures scattered in the park was most certainly planned out according to an iconographic program, now lost. Beside the usual mythological or allegorical themes appear the strange little monkeys, or rustic subjects such as beggars or peasants, or mannerist inventions like the boar spitting water and the peasant with the barrel, borrowed from the phantasmagoric repertoires of Buontalenti's Boboli and Pratolino Gardens.

At the dawn of the neoclassic period, Ottaviano Diodati, an aristocrat from Lucca, reorganized the waterworks, added some new statues and planned new plantings in the initial parterre. Owing to the great fame of Collodi Gardens, Charles VII of Naples gave Diodati a commission for the royal palace of Caserta (which he did not fulfil), and in 1793, King Stanislas Poniatovsky of Poland asked the Garzonis to send him a drawing of the villa and of the exuberant, eccentric rococo shooting lodge designed by Filippo Juvarra.

After the Garzonis, Collodi was inherited by the Paravicinos, and then belonged to the Poschi-Meurons, the Giacominis, and finally to the Gardis, who are dedicated guardians of this important and demanding patrimony.

Built at the side of the area where its park unfolds, Villa Garzoni is one place where the baroque style triumphs. Behind the villa is concealed the sumptuous rococo shooting lodge built in the eighteenth century by Filippo Juvarra.

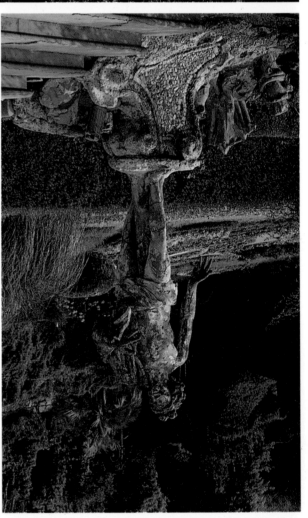

Previous pages: An aerial view of the park's architectural score, shaped by deep terraces along the side of the hill. Opposite: Sculpted in stone or terracotta, the statues of the park once expressed a determined iconographic program, which has now been lost. Above: The suggestive grotto of Neptune shows its heritage in the mannerist artistic language.

After the multicolored initial parterre,
the ascentional play of stairways begins,
punctuated by several grottoes inhabited
by statues.

Opposite: Dominated by an allegorical
statue representing Fame, the top
fountain overlooks the whole park.

Royal Villa of Marlia, now Pecci-Blunt Villa Marlia (Lucca)

Here, out of the darkness, the yew tree weaves the vague order of its greenness to make the pleasant theater, which is mirrored in the lake.

This is how Francesco Franceschi, a Lucchese versifier of the eighteenth century, describes the famous open-air theater of Marlia. The villa was built in 1778 for Prince-Count Wenzel Anton von Kaunitz-Rietberg, who was chancellor for Maria Theresa of Austria, and a keen connoisseur of the art of gardening, ever since the empress had given him the gardens previously belonging to Countess von Schulemburg, in the outskirts of Vienna. Created in the second half of the seventeenth century, the original formal gardens of Marlia had belonged to the Counts Orsetti since 1651, and were a blend of mannerist reminiscences, which foreshadowed the solemn, controlled baroque style of the Versailles of Louis XIV.

In an unchallenged position of command at the edge of a vast lawn, the residential building stands out, exalted by its limpid volumes, and aristocratically isolated from the arboreal side-scenes. Two uninterrupted, wall-like hedges accompany the development of the enormous lawn, ending in the hemicycle behind the villa, where a sumptuous water theater, eighteenth-century evocation of the mannerist nymphaeum, ends up in a grotto fountain.

At Marlia, all extreme effects are banned, unlike the clamorous baroque ornamentations, both refined and naïve, of the neighboring Villa Collodi. Here too, the long fishpond, with its surrounding court of well-ordered lemon containers, is crowned by an exedra-nymphaeum. From there, across a circular vestibule surrounding a basin, is the sophisticated open-air theater, perhaps the most perfect in the whole of Italy. The theater was planted in 1652, a soft and harmonious alternation of full but nevertheless light volumes, with carved niches now inhabited by eighteenth-century terra-cotta characters from the Commedia dell'Arte. A few pine trees and cypresses boldly emerge above the horizontal score of the hedges, while nature in its free state is exiled to the "wild" landscape at the back of the two water theaters, and behind the villa and the lemon basin.

It may have been this *esprit de géométrie* that attracted Elisa Baciocchi. This ambitious sister of Napoleon, Princess of Lucca, was in search of a summer residence worthy of her small but showy court, and she obliged Count Orsetti to sell her the estate for half a million francs in silver. With his pungent Tuscan sense of humor, the count had the metal melted down and turned into a sumptuous dinner set, which he is said to have exhibited through the streets of Lucca on a cart, finally stopping under Elisa's windows, having daringly invited her to come and see "the Marlia Villa pass by."

The Princess felt constrained in the narrow horizons of her principality, in the drowsy atmosphere of a provincial city that had been famous for centuries mainly as a *ville d'eau*, and her ambitions resulted in the renovation of the villa park after English romantic models. The village of Bagni di Lucca, visited by famous foreigners since Monsieur de Montaigne had come there in 1581, received a new architectural garb, mainly thanks to Nottolini's activity, inaugurating a cosmopolitan, intellectual nineteenth century, with visitors like Byron, Shelley, Stendhal, the Brownings, and Heinrich Heine.

Elisa's building furor also fell upon Marlia, where copses and a small lake were introduced, as well as new species of trees. Despite the difficulties of water supply, tulips started blooming, and weeping willows, the *Gingko biloba*, thujas, and mimosas started growing. Nothing seemed capable of stopping the princess, although the Lucca countryside "divided and subdivided both in the plain and in the hills, patiently tilled meter after meter, would never have toned in with this far too violent insertion, completely alien to it with its fake naturalism," as Isa Belli Barsali remarks.

The collapse of the Napoleonic empire and the arrival of the British occupation troops in 1814 put an end to Elisa's short reign, preventing her scheduled destruction of the baroque parts of the gardens. Thus, in 1817, Marlia passed into the hands of the Bourbon-Parmas, then to the Princes of Capua. In 1923, it was bought by Count and Countess Pecci-Blunt. Anna Laetitia Pecci-Blunt, a sensitive patron of artists and mediatrix of the European avant-gardes in the Italian cultural spheres, devoted all her careful ministerings to this splendid Tuscan park, giving new life to its intermingled baroque and classical graces.

Property of the Counts Orsetti as early as 1651, the Marlia Gardens blend late mannerist aspects with baroque and French tastes. Here, the neoclassic period found an ideal humus, by virtue of the important works promoted by the new proprietor of the villa, the ambitious Elisa Bonaparte Baciocchi. The stylistic precedents she set were quickly followed throughout the province of Lucca.

The formal but soft side-scenes of the open-air theater date back to 1652. Among the greenery, characters of the eighteenth-century Commedia dell'Arte recite their dialogues. According to Elisa Baciocchi's designs, the formal garden was to be entirely destroyed, to be replaced by a neoclassical, romantic creation resembling that of the imperial architect Berthault. Napoleon's defeat and the arrival of the British occupants fortunately put a stop to this project.

The fish ponds, fountains, and secret garden, with the usual walls decorated with pebbles, punctuated by pilasters in rustic ashlar, date from the original eighteenth-century design.

A customary feature of the baroque garden, water plays an important part here in a context of geometric elegance that brings to mind French sources of inspiration.

Villa Mansi
Segromigno in Monte (Lucca)

Whereas nowadays the conservation of the past or, whenever necessary, an intelligent, non-intrusive restoration has become a capital imperative, in the past one style followed the other and often deliberately destroyed its predecessor. The concept of the assertion of novelty at the expense of the past, through an appropriation of roles and spaces, did not provide for the cohabitation of consecutive artistic languages. This was not only the case for buildings in the city streets, or in interior decoration, but the aspect of the parks also changed according to fashion, being remodeled every time by total or partial destruction of the previous design. This explains why anybody going to Villa Mansi at Segromigno hoping to admire the baroque layout of the one garden created by Filippo Juvarra would be disappointed. And a similar disillusionment would await anyone looking for the transformations commissioned at the end of the sixteenth century by the Benedettis, or later, by the Cenamis, who owned the place before the Mansis, who arrived there in 1675.

The Mansis were important members of the local aristocracy, wealthy and learned, who had gained great power through various lucrative trades. Praised by Franceschini, one of numerous Lucchese scholars, the villa underwent its last transformation in 1742, when Abbot Giovan Francesco Giusti had its graceful baroque façade built. Designed by Juvarra between 1725 and 1732, the park followed French canons, embellished by parterres of trimmed box hedges, a *pavillon d'horloge*, and enlivened by the inevitable waterworks. Very little remains of the original creation—only part of a watercourse that disappears underground, later to reappear and flow into the large balustraded fishpond, decorated with eight large mythological figures, among which stand out a few pots of red geraniums. Even an element like the ruins of Diana's grotto, which might at first sight be associated with the early romantic taste for ruins, is merely an Arcadian vestige of the eighteenth-century intervention.

In spite of the villa's famous baroque lineage, the present park is characterized by its almost completely romantic atmosphere. The nineteenth-century design of the garden can also be seen in the neighboring Villa Torrigiani, and it is common in the entire province of Lucca, where the interest in botany has always been keen, as evidenced by the brightly colored baroque gardens, and enhanced after Elisa's reign and the European fame of the local Bagni (Spas). The romantic park develops among the formal designs, between flowerbeds in whose magic circle luxurious corollas throng, between the *rocailles* and the theatrical statues, permeating everything in a triumphal march. It proceeds with such impetus that it sweeps away whole parts of genial baroque and rococo decoration. The Lucchese passion for new floral and botanical fashions is such that what does not exist is created: to satisfy the most demanding collectors, a hybridation center was created near Lucca, born of the aristocracy's maniacal love for the romantic flower par excellence, the camellia (but also extending to gardenias, peonies, palm trees, and rare conifers). On the one hand, the international contacts established with floriculturists and botanists by the Lucchese mercantile oligarchy favored the introduction of new varieties of exotic flowers; on the other, the particular nature of the soil in that part of Tuscany explains the successful development in Italy of *Camellia japonica*. A fairly stable temperature, with little difference between minimum and maximum, combined with a damp, cool soil, constituted the ideal humus for that type of cultivation. Another offspring of the romantic mood is the bamboo copse (*Phyllostachys nigra*) which, together with the alley of palm trees (*Trachycarpus fortunei*), accompanies the small bridge leading to the villa; these echoes from the Orient blend with the exotic atmosphere created by the Japanese palm trees (*Musa japonica*) planted in a semicircle around the fishpond at the back of the house. This exoticism is also expressed by the Atlas cedar, which began arriving in Europe in the middle of the nineteenth century, and the Californian cypress, in combination with the ilexes of the eighteenth-century gardens. *Liriodendron tulipifera* were successfully cultivated by the keen Lucchese aristocrats, taking advantage of the damp climate that suited the camellias so well. Indeed, a special touch is added to the Marlia park by the majestic bearing of a group of nine, very ancient liriodendron, at least forty meters high. The visitor is all the more impressed when, in summer, the long blossoming branches sweep down to the ground, and he will not forget this bewitching sight.

Property of the Benedettis, the Cenamis, and of the Mansis (from 1675 onwards), the villa is said to be haunted by the ghost of Lucida Mansi, guilty of having sold her soul to the devil. The last transformation of the villa was made in 1742 by the architect Giovan Francesco Giusti. The formal park was entirely created by Filippo Juvarra, the most prominent landscape architect of the period between the late baroque and rococo. Here, eight mythological stone figures watch over the fish pond, which is entirely surrounded by a balustrade.

Above and opposite: Among the garden elements dating from the nineteenth century transformation of the park, some baroque pieces persist: the statues, the small fountains, and the whimsical stepped watercourse that sometimes appears, sometimes disappears underground.

Torrigiani Gardens
Camigliano (Lucca)

Just as the gardens of Villa Garzoni at Collodi had deserved Sbarra's praises, the park of Villa Torrigiani at Camigliano di Lucca inspired a vivid ode from Cerati, a local chronicler, who recalls its Wind Grotto which, in the baroque manner, marked the end of Flora's Garden. Indeed, the still-sumptuous remnants of what was, at the end of the seventeenth century, an enchanted garden, a jewel-case for the rarest colors, still constitute the centerpiece of the present Torrigiani park.

The garden is designed on two levels—a long fishpond with a balustrade and mythological statues, and, to the south, an embanked area which used to be the seat of the floral collection and waterworks. Following the demise of the rare botanical collections, the garden has been remodeled with fewer fanciful flowerbeds. These small patches of ground once used to harbor teeming microcosms of color so disruptive and baroque that only simple, humble stones could dam them up.

At a time when the way of life of the refined local lords, both Lucchese and Florentine, was pervaded with French influences, the immoderate love for rare, refined things could not but seize the infinitely seductive opportunities a garden offered for collecting. The sumptuous orchestration of balustrades, the double flights of steps, were but a symphonic prelude, a transition towards the paradise of the trees, flowers, and heady fragrances. At least this was the case in one part of the garden, where architecture left the upper hand to nature's opulent, swarming, if controlled, strength. This point of view certainly contrasted with the classical typology of the late-baroque landscape, which stressed the architectural component, central on the whole territory.

However, Le Notre's dictates arrived in Italy too, imported by Jean de la Quintinie's treatise *Instructions pour les Jardins fruitiers et potagers* (Instructions for fruit and vegetable Gardens). In accordance with this text, translated into Italian in 1730, the architect Domenico Martini designed a scenic parterre, embroidered with hedges, visible from the distant cypress alley. Martini planted a splendid collection of camellias on the far side of the villa, where there was a small, mannerist, "wild" wood. Today, unfortunately, the structure of this baroque park is only a memory.

In 1816, Vittoria Saltini, last heir of Niccolò Cesare Saltini who had bought the villa in 1651, married Marquess Pietro Guadagni Torrigiani. In the wake of the enthusiasm raised by Elisa Baciocchi's impressive works at Marlia, a new neoclassic, early romantic stamp was impressed upon the park. Thus, the thick colors, the exasperated, lace-like shapes of the baroque flora gave way to the romantic gardenias and camellias, and the magnolias with their white lotuses floating on the dark, translucent green of the leaves. This can still be admired along the north side of the villa, suffused in the tangle of the nineteenth-century camellia copses. Some exotic trees, *lusitanica* and *macrocarpa* cypresses, *Liriodendron tulipifera* and *Gingko biloba* with its fan-shaped leaves, mix with bay oaks, Lebanon cedars, ancient ilexes, plane trees, lime trees, and *Taxodium distichum*. The pink *Camellia japonica*, the freshness of the

Magnolia soulangeana are accompanied by the *Camellia rubra simplex*, 'Orfeo' and 'Virginia Franco', and dwarf species. This whole world contrasts with the secret necromancy of the grotto, hidden under the wide flights of steps, where water effects and monstrous figures used to frighten visitors.

Free from fashion and period, relying on its importance and "political" impact, the cypress alley cuts a dominant figure and solemnly leads the way to the villa—a linear axis straight to the magnificent house, framed-in by austere conifers. The villa and the park today belong to Princess Colonna Torrigiani, direct descendant of Marquess Pietro Guadagni Torrigiani, whose botanical fervor she has also inherited.

Designed by Muzio Oddi, the eighteenth-century villa is characterized by its two elegant trefoil loggias in the Serlio style. Praised by Cerati, an eighteenth-century poet from Lucca, it belongs to the Princess Colonna Torrigiani.

Previous pages: Sardonic masks, mermaids, the diversified, theatrical movement of the stairs, grottoes, and fountains, the definitive volumes of the box trees, are all that remains of the original baroque features of the garden.

Above and opposite: In the top part of the garden, which is divided into two zones— the first more architectural, and the second dedicated to the floral collections—the attention is focused on a long fish pond guarded by a mythological statue and enlivened by balustrades.

Villa Roncioni
Pugnano (Pisa)

Between 1773 and 1779 Francesco Roncioni commissioned the architect Giuseppe Gaetano Nicolai to transform the building that a 1592 chronicle called *casa grande*. The Roncionis had laid the first foundations of the present architectural complex as early as 1468, when they bought "a plot of land with small farmhouses," at the foot of Mount Pisano. Whereas the residential building, a central part with two lateral wings, has more ordinary and traditional features, the gardens became a place of architectural experimentation, which foreshadowed the nodal points of artistic debate in the first half of the nineteenth century.

In the case of Villa Roncioni, more than a proper garden, one may speak of a space devoted to containing architectural objects, varying in their function and language. The most impressive and articulate of these folies is the neo-gothic silkworm farm built in 1826 by the Pisan architect Alessandro Gherardesca. The building included a silk mill on the ground floor and, on the top floor, rooms where the silkworms were bred—the Roncioni family traded in silk. The building is an up-to-date example of gothic revival architecture without sharing the more theatrical inclinations of this stylistic trend. Gherardesca prefers the social aspirations and technological innovations of English early-industrialist architecture rather than the luxurious, ogival phantasies of Horace Walpole's Strawberry Hill.

The Roncionis eagerly followed the rapid economic transformations happening at that time in Europe, and their social concern was seconded by the architect, who offered the silk workers an atmosphere with more light and more space, where life was more tolerable. According to Gherardesca's ideals, "a grandiose picture with the various cultivations that deck the picturesque mountain slopes, with the contiguous wood and orderly garden" was composed. A hermitage, a chapel, and a nymphaeum followed suit in the park vegetation. In the chapel, built in 1846, the architect still demonstrates a certain taste for gothic elements, but also makes use of local canons, drawing inspiration from the Santa Maria della Spina church in Pisa, and using the recomposed fragments of a fourteenth-century three-lighted window to decorate the spire.

With its austere, measured quotations, this theoretical position was quite different from the creative impulse of some of Gherardesca's contemporaries—Pelagio Palagi and the Sienese Agostino Fantastici for instance—or from the imaginative freedom of the English romanticism, interpreted by Giuseppe Jappelli. Gherardesca's project was rather in the tradition of the industrial gothic of the Rossi Gardens, at Schio, created by Alessandro Caregaro Negrin.

Having drained the medievalizing vein, for the nymphaeum—devoted to recreation and pleasure—the architect opted for a neoclassic synthesis, contaminated from the inside by an amused revisitation of the mannerist grotto. The simple layout of sculptures and semi-columns around a wide central arch, a discreet tribute to Schinkel's poetics, contrasts with the picturesque *rocailles* inside. But since the decoration is not supported by a sophisticated iconographic program—although it uses the usual rustic mosaics, small, shell-shaped marble fountains, and artificial or natural concretions—it fails to evoke the mysterious essence that vibrated in the bewitched grottoes of the end of the sixteenth century.

Built by Giuseppe Gaetano Nicolai between 1773 and 1779 on the spot where a sixteenth century casa grande *once stood, the simple architecture of the villa stands out against the wood that decks the slopes of Mount Pisano.*

One contribution of the English landscaped garden is the will to unite the garden, the neighboring cultivated fields, *and the contiguous wood into a single landscape picture.*

Opposite: Built by Alessandro Gherardesca, a Pisan architect, the grotto, or nymphaeum, is a revival of the neoclassic language, with slight traces of Schinkel's influence.
Right: The romantic park is also nourished by classical signs, such as this sarcophagus.
Bottom: Inside the grotto is a display of the usual ornamental repertoire of rocailles, mineral and artificial concretions, and small fountains in the form of nautiluses.

Following pages: Behind the flat area of the garden, with its bushes of Chamaerops humilis *and its typically Tuscan lemon pots, rises another of Gherardesca's creations, the neo-gothic Silkworm Farm built in 1926, certainly the most impressive building of the park.*

Castle of Uzzano
Greve (Florence)

In his treatise *Dell'edificar delle case e palazzi in villa e dell'ordinar dei giardini e orti* (On the Edification of Houses and Palaces in Villas and on the Arrangement of Gardens big and small), written between 1580 and 1590, Giovanni Sanminiati describes the advantages of country life, especially underlining "the whiling away of time in pleasant debates or musics or other such entertainments and retiring to philosophize in those moments when company is lacking." Uzzano has retained its double function as a place for aristocratic functions and a center of agricultural production.

Surrounded by a host of pale, well trained olive trees, an orderly army of vineyards, and the black ink of the cypresses, Uzzano is inserted in the ordered countryside of the Chianti region. This light blue, neoplatonic landscape has almost become the essential exemplification of the humanists' anthropocentric ideal, thanks to centuries of careful ministerings. Scenery of a dream, fed by the very ornamental and architectural elements that animate it, Uzzano is a faithful reflection of the Italian garden poetics.

After belonging to the Uzzano family (one of whose members, Niccolò, was made famous in a Donatello bust), the castle belonged to the Masettis da Bagnano, then to the Castelbarco Albani Masettis, who still own it today. Built around the year 1000, the castle took on its present villa aspect in the first half of the seventeenth century, when the patrician building was completely restructured, and an early-baroque garden was created. Impressive excavation works completely remodeled the outline of the hill, creating a gradual slope of terraces, linked together by spectacular flights of steps, with the slender verticality of cypresses as a counterpoint.

This garden is a place for metamorphoses, where the pagan stone and terra-cotta statues placidly allow the ivy to deck them, or fleetingly emerge from the geometric volumes of the box hedges. The space strives to unite the seduction of baroque chaos with the rarefied order of the Renaissance. Glimpses of landscape extend the compact thread of the cypresses, maritime pines, and Atlas and Lebanon cedars, all planted at the end of the nineteenth century.

Leaving the secular wistaria that covers the castle, the visitor proceeds down to the two symmetrical basins that separate the raised labyrinth from the open-air amphitheater. From there, an alley of cypresses winds its way into a wood, an early-romantic addition of English inspiration, which conceals some roses, azaleas, camellias, and rhododendrons. More flowers—zinnias, geraniums, and roses—color the flowerbeds that punctuate the way up to the castle, flanked with a lemon-house, a common feature of Tuscan patrician houses.

Built around the year 1000 on the hills of Greve in Chianti, the castle of Uzzano stands out against the box tree volutes of the parterre, beyond a tall cedar.

Views of the Uzzano Gardens, a baroque creation that retains the Tuscan Renaissance passion for a radiant geometry.

Bottom: Molded in Impruneta terra-cotta, a statue representing Spring stands out against the compact texture of the hedges that form the labyrinth.

Transformed into a sumptuous residence in the first half of the seventeenth century, Uzzano is built on a hill that was remodeled into a terraced garden. The formal garden is accompanied by nineteenth-century romantic touches, such as the wood and the numerous trees, mainly Atlas and Lebanon cedars, planted at the end of the nineteenth century.

Villa Medici of Castello
Sesto Fiorentino (Florence)

The close relationship between certain Tuscan villas and the landscape that surrounds them is evidence of the historicization of the landscape, where history becomes a form of nature that reflects its image. Evidence of this can be found in the fourteen lunettes which the Flemish Giusto Utens painted in 1599 in the grand duke's villa at Artimino, rather than in actual landscapes which have often been severely altered.

The villa at Castello, a small town near Florence, is besieged by an industrial development on one side, while on its left, behind the walls of the villa, the outline of the hills and the rows of cypresses have not changed since Giovanni and Lorenzo di Pierfrancesco de' Medici acquired the villa and estate in 1477. This landscape had already had a well-defined outline for a century, as the merchant Giovanni Morelli tells us at the end of the fourteenth century: "All around, as a garland, slopes and hills that can be climbed; and also big, high mountains not less pleasant to watch . . . Near the houses you see domestic fields, well tilled ans adorned with fruits and most beautiful vines and a great number of wells and courses of water."

When Giovanni il Popolano died, Caterina Sforza inherited the property, and after her, their son, Giovanni dalle Bande Nere, who had spent his childhood there. After Cosimo I became Duke of Florence, Niccolò Pericoli, called Tribolo, was commissioned to reorganize both the house and the garden. On an ambitious iconologic program imagined by Benedetto Varchi to glorify the ducal pomp, a building was erected that cut the previously uninterruped axis extending from the long entrance alley, past Venus's labyrinth in the center of the gardens, past the grotto, to end up at the fishpond on the top level. Tribolo was replaced at the head of the works by Vasari, seconded by Ammannati and Giambologna.

Imprisoned in box hedges, the formal garden was dedicated to ornamental and eulogistic functions. The central fountain was designed by Tribolo and built around 1546, dominated by Ammannati's sculptural group representing Hercules causing Antaeus to burst—an allusion to Cosimo's triumph over his enemies. The fountain was meant to collect the waters of the other fountains situated on the garden slopes, an illustration of the perfect organization of the Tuscan water supply and of the new era of peace and prosperity, thanks to which Florence received an abundance of fruit from every city in the state. The grotto opens up in the platform that supports the big basin at the top of the gardens. With its *rocailles* and motionless, mannerist statues representing animals, it is a reflection of the supernatural, magic bestiary of the *Wunderkammer*. Mineral, maritime, and animal elements, stalactites, artificial concretions, friezes, mosaics, and large shell masks, three basins by Ammannati teeming with an alarming multitude of Giambologna's stone and bronze animals, almost concealed in the damp darkness—a whole universe is dominated by the mythical unicorn, once more meant to represent Cosimo. Every single element, geometric flowerbeds, rich borders, the variety of levels and *coups de théâtre*, the top basin with its grotesque and tormented bronze giant representing Winter (or The Apennine), by Ammannati, standing out against the agitated green of the "wild" landscape,

everything contributes to demonstrating the concept cherished by mannerism—the improvement of nature through human artifice. An idea that was to be codified by Vincenzo Danti in his *Trattato delle perfette proporzioni*, dedicated to Cosimo I: "Order can be more perfect in art than in nature, since man, being acquainted with the imperfection of natural things, can avoid them or treat them, thus coming next to perfection."

Cosimo's golden period faded away, and Buontalenti doubled the body of the house and inserted an ashlared portal. In the seventeenth century the villa became the favorite residence of Cardinal Giovan Carlo, a sensual man, and a great supporter of melodrama, who probably devoted himself—as did the Lorraines who occupied the throne after the Medicis' extinction—to the collection of citrus fruits which, in their large basins of Impruneta terra-cotta, give the garden their fragrance and color. Some six hundred species are still kept in the garden—oranges, bergamots, citrons, lemons, hybrid and anomalous varieties that continue to tell of the grand dukes' botanical pride in Jacopo Ligozzi's paintings.

Owners of the villa since 1477, the Medici is called on the best architects of the time to supervise the building of the villa and its park: Tribolo was followed by Vasari, seconded by Ammannati and Giambologna, and finally by Buontalenti, who designed the ashlared portal in the center of the façade.

Previous pages: A comprehensive view of the Castello gardens, outlined by geometric hedges among which stand the lemon pots. The garden was reorganized at the end of the eighteenth century according to the wishes of Grand Duke Pietro Leopoldo of Lorraine.

Opposite: The mannerist grotto is decorated with rocailles in polychrome stone and shells. The two basins are attributed to Ammannati, and the animal statues belong to Giambologna's repertoire.

Florence

Fallani Garden

Between 1865 and 1871, the drowsy city of Florence assumed—almost against its own will—the role of capital of the young Italian kingdom. As a local answer to the bloodless Piedmontese "colonization", the Macchiaioli—who met at the Caffè Michelangelo—adopted a new pictorial language to express a "Tuscanity" that stubbornly refused to disappear. This style of painting, an impression of reality represented by the means of colored spots, of lights and shades, is also tinged with social implications. Among the most refined and most European of the macchiaiolo group, Silvestro Lega and Telemaco Signorini often set the terse, uneventful routine of their narration against a background of peaceful, secluded bourgeois gardens.

On the other hand, the architect Giuseppe Poggi upheld the opposite thesis and, on the strength of his faith in a new golden age for the city, expressed himself in an eulogistic idiom that was not exempt from international influences, and aimed at reviving the grandiloquent stylistic features of the sixteenth century. Interpreting the new exigencies of Florence, capital of the House of Savoy, he conceived the most significant works of expansion and urban planning. Thus were born the ring road, airy boulevards that replaced the ancient walls, the hill promenade, and the panoramic belvedere of Piazzale Michelangelo. The key point of the remodeling of this area was the Piazza della Mulina, which now bears Poggi's name.

Not far from this square, a dense curtain of buildings facing the medieval San Nicolo street conceals a garden that seems to sum up the ambitious aspirations of the new Florence, in apparent contrast with the limited, private aura of the Macchiaioli's world. Unexpectedly, after a vaulted inner passage, one comes upon the elliptic graveled area that constitutes the first level of this garden, the design of which is markedly ascentional.

The impressionist charm of the wisteria that covers the house also suffuses the sides of the small amphitheater. The first terrace is a kind of romantic nymphaeum, in the center of which rises the one liquid element of the garden, a fountain, dominated by a slender bronze youth, created at the end of the nineteenth century by the Neapolitan sculptor Renda.

Along the slopes, after a first attempt at containing the untidy elegance of the Tuscan bush with symmetrical box hedges and vast walls of ivy, the following terraces are laid out in a disorder that appears casual, but is really the result of a carefully planned design. Introduced to mark an itinerary among the greenness are some elements taken from the contemporary urban furniture, such as spherical, cast iron streetlamps, neo-classic urns, and numerous benches that offer rest in the shade.

In the center of a wider space marked by a circular stone seat, behind which grows a thick copse of bamboo, a crouching faun bears a lamp on his back, resembling a kind of modernist Telamon. The straight progression of a wide grassy path, punctuated by alternating walnut trees, fig trees, and cypresses, refrains the exuberant vegetation that hugs the medieval city's mighty walls. From the garden, steep steps lead to one of the towers that dot those city walls. There, the view encompasses all the roofs, domes and cupolas, towers and church towers, the tall loggias of Florence, before moving on to the soft outline of the Fiesole and Settignano hills, and finally rests upon the comforting, serene sight of Mount Morello.

Concealed at the foot of the tower, a grotto encloses a luminous sculpture by Roberto Fallani, emblematically entitled Biological Mutations. This presence synthesizes the alchemic, empiric tension of Tuscan mannerism and the scientific inclinations of nineteenth-century positivism.

An impressionistic view of the garden, where the ivy mixes with the cascading wisteria that decks the house.

Opposite and above: The ascentional development of the garden follows the slope of the ground. Cast iron street lamps and other ornamental elements further increase the sense of the nineteenth century.

Following pages: From the garden the visitor can reach one of the towers that punctuate the surrounding walls, and enjoy an extraordinary view of Florence and its surrounding hills.

Villa La Pietra
Florence

After the war, I felt the urge to go back to Florence, where I had first lived. The impressions of childhood were all the more acute for being rediscovered after an absence so dense with events. While I was gazing at the city from the garden of my villa at La Pietra, I felt my former interests surge up inside me, stronger than ever. All at once the whole valley, with the Duomo in the middle, started shining under a shower of golden rain. At that very moment the past became present.

With these words, taken from the preface of his 1938 edition of his marvelous book *Gli ultimi Medici* (The Last Medici), Sir Harold Acton, a famous English scholar and writer who spent his youth in China before setting down for the rest of his life in Italy, faithfully conjures up the atmosphere of his La Pietra gardens on the old road to Bologna. Perhaps Sir Acton was inspired by the house—whose vastness is the only remnant of the 1460 Renaissance building—perhaps he even followed the traces left by Francesco Sassetti, Lorenzo the Magnificent's banker, and the first known owner of the villa, when he wrote his studies on the last splendors of the Medici family. In any case, at La Pietra, he gathered around himself a brilliant intellectual circle, one of the exclusive microcosms around which the "Italianated" Anglo-American cultural elite gravitated in the first half of the twentieth century. With a certain candid *naïveté*, sometimes with a sense of complete renouncement and painful extraneousness, they seemed to feel an urge to immerse themselves in a golden past of ideal beauty and elegance, a past echoed by the quaint rooms of the Stibbert Museum and in the pages of Henry James and Edith Wharton.

The other stars of the constellation of privileged residences, on the Tuscan hills, were Lady Sybil Cutting's Medici Villa, Bernard Berenson's Tatti (with a garden designed by Cecil Pinsent), Montegufoni, where Osbert Sitwell and his eccentric brothers commissioned Severini to paint a cycle of frescoes, Strong's Balze and Vernon Lee's Palmerino, which set young Mario Praz dreaming when he was in Florence. These patrons played a fundamental part in restoring their villas to their original states, lost after centuries of disfiguring alterations. So did Sir Arthur, father of the author of *Memoirs for an Aesthete*, who bought the villa at the very beginning of the twentieth century and brought the garden back to its original terraced form, canceling the picturesque romantic version ordered by the Prussian ambassador, who had resided at La Pietra in the nineteenth century. The vaguely delineated wood cut down, the shape of the hill was remodeled into the former terraces—documented by drawings kept at the Uffizi—and Sir Arthur reintroduced the noble, sophisticated features that suited the graceful and discreet baroque perspective attributed to Carlo Fontana, datable from the first half of the seventeenth century. Enlivened by fountains and myrtle hedges, the three levels are linked together by sinuous flights of stairs and balustrades. While it belonged to the Capponis, the garden had been enlarged, and its true baroque character springs from the articulated succession of its elements, but also from a search for strong contrasts of light and shade, suspended in the stillness of the geometric darkness.

The only element of the first garden that has not been contaminated by the successive changes is the apple orchard: facing the vast, lush lemon-house, it is a proper fifteenth-century treasure, a *hortus conclusus* surrounded by precious walls, decorated with polychrome stones and tiles. It is impossible not to be reminded of the learned, private dimension of the frescoes painted by Ghirlandaio on the walls of the Sassetti Chapel, in the church of Santa Maria Novella.

Today, as Sir Harold Acton stipulated in his will, the park and villa belong to the University of New York.

Covered with pink *banksiae*, pervaded with a dark coolness, the alley seems to be a background set for the first performance of a melodrama (a genre born in early-baroque Florence); and converses with the radiant luminosity of a Corinthian colonnade. Looking like so many terse open-air drawing rooms, sunlit clearings open up between dark, sumptuous walls of ilexes and cypresses; they are inhabited by Orazio Marinali's and Bonazza's statues, brought here from the Venetian Parnassus of the Brenta villas.

Built in the first half of the seventeenth century and characterized by a restrained baroque taste, the façade of Villa La Pietra is attributed to Carlo Fontana. The owner, Sir Harold Acton, a historian and writer, bequeathed the villa to the University of New York when he died.

*Previous pages: Views of the garden.
Above: A bright portico of humanistic
inspiration recalls the first period of the
villa's existence, when it belonged to
Francesco Sassetti, banker for Lorenzo
the Magnificent and a client
of Ghirlandaio.*

*Opposite: Statues by Orazio Marinali
and Bonazza bring a Venetian note into
the Tuscan essence of the garden. Box
hedges and walls create a succession
of open-air chambers.*

Villa Medici of Pratolino
Pratolino (Florence)

The mannerist garden, an alternation of geometric hedges and wild ravines, with labyrinths and strange waterworks, a lair for giants and automatons, an alchemic laboratory of metamorphosis, is the scene for a strenuous dialectical confrontation between nature and art. Contrivances borrowed from the experiments of the sixteenth-century theater—a privileged forge of inventions meant to nourish the mannerist taste for deceit—such as mobile devices, architectural or vegetal side-scenes, deceptive machineries to inflate spaces, all find a new and more lasting purpose in the parks of villas, shooting lodges, and palaces.

From Francesco I de' Medici with his private study, to alchemist-Emperor Rudolf II of Hapsburg, the princes of the time enshrined a host of preciously eccentric objects, of rare, extravagant joys, whimsical triumphs of shells, corals, rock crystals, coconuts, and ostrich eggs mounted in gold and silver. This universe flowed down the princes' shelves, and out of their cabinets, to populate the grottoes, supernatural folies, and labyrinthine itineraries of the disquieting mannerist garden.

Bernardo Buontalenti—the most important architect and an eminent representative of the Florentine artistic and cultural spheres in the second half of the sixteenth century—was often called upon by the Medicis to build or remodel the parks of their residences. After his first appearance at Boboli, where, after Tribolo's death in 1550, Vasari and Bandinelli, then Bartolomeo Ammannati had worked before him, Buontalenti worked *ex novo* at Artimino, Poggiofrancoli, and Pratolino, and redesigned ancient estates belonging to the grand dukes, such as Magia, Lappeggi, Cerreto Guidi, la Petraia, and Castello.

Pratolino, a vast palace in Vignola's manner, was built between 1568 and 1586 by Bernardo Buontalenti for Francesco I de' Medici and his Venetian lover, Bianca Cappello—who became grand duchess in 1578— and was finished under Ferdinando I. Destroyed under the Lorraines, it became the property of the Russian princes Demidoff, and was finally alienated in 1955 by the last heir, Maria.

The late-mannerist building was sumptuous and rich with architectural inventions, but the great marvel was the park. This is how Montaigne describes it in 1580 in his *Voyage en Italie*:

> There is an extraordinary grotto composed of a great many niches and rooms, inlaid and made everywhere of a mineral that is said to be extracted from certain mountains, held together by invisible nails. With the action of the water, not only musics and harmonies are created, but various movements are imparted to statues and doors, innumerable animals that dive in to drink and other such things.

Pratolino was supplied with water by a two-mile-long aqueduct, and since water was abundant, it was used for a number of quaint effects:

> When you move a single device, the whole grotto fills with water: all the seats spurt water onto your buttocks, and if you run away up the steps to the castle, every second step a thousand jets squirt out, that soak you until you reach the top of the structure. And further: At the foot of the castle, there is, among other things, an alley fifty feet wide and fifty feet long. . . . On both sides, every fifth or tenth step, certain long, most beautiful freestone parapets, at whose level some small fountains spurt out of the walls; in this manner, the whole alley becomes a succession of water jets. At the end, a pretty fountain pours its water into a large basin through a marble statue representing a woman doing her washing; she is wringing a towel of white marble, from which water drips down and underneath, there is a second basin that seems filled with boiling water for the washing.

The enchantments of this "Garden of Armida" seemed to be endless: "And they are building the body of a giant with an eye cavity that is three cubits wide," wrote Monsieur de Montaigne's secretary. This colossal statue of the Apennine, new divinity of the mannerist pantheon, created by Giambologna, and which concealed a secret room in its head, still testifies today to Buontalenti's grandiose conception.

Similar inventions would never have been possible in Villa Careggi, where Cosimo the Ancient received Platonic humanists, nor at Poggio a Caiano, where Lorenzo the Magnificent gathered the poets of the *certame coronario* (royal poetic contest). Dominated by Baccio Bandinelli's Jupiter, which overhangs the ideal line of access to the villa, Pratolino seems to have been built on purpose to receive, at the very end of the seventeenth century, Grand Prince Ferdinando, son of the austere Cosimo III, with his picturesque gangs of the *recitar cantando* virtuosos.

In this magic garden, against the background of Cupid's grotto, in front of the fishpond of the Mask, or the Frog basin, the Paduan harpsichord player Bartolomeo Cristofori, a music teacher and an innovator, would seek inspiration and entertain his aristocratic host. A strange, unfortunate character who sought refuge at Pratolino to soothe his melancholy temper, Prince Ferdinando, aged sixteen, had one of his musical works performed under the aegis of Mount Parnassus. Its ambitious title, in Marini's manner, was *Colla forza d'amor si vince amore* (Love is vanquished by the strength of love).

In the center of a seven-square-mile estate north of Florence, Pratolino was built between 1568 and 1586 by Buontalenti for Francesco I de' Medici.

*The Mugnone fountain (bottom right),
the fish pond of the Mask (bottom left),
Bandinelli by Baccio
Bandinelli's Jupiter (top); and above all,
Giambologna's colossal Apennine
(opposite) all bear witness to the
metamorphic pomp of the mannerist
garden.*

Opposite: The neoclassical style of the Demidoff Villa seen through the greenery of the "wilderness".
Above: The present park is but a shadow of the marvels that used to abound there.

In this Pompei of mannerism, the visitor may come across fragments of statues; those belonging to the original statue of the Apennine are enormous.

La Gamberaia
Settignano (Florence)

This is probably the most perfect example of a great effect obtained on a small scale.

Thus spoke Edith Wharton in 1909, referring to the famous Italian gardens of Villa Gamberaia at Settignano. The present layout is the result of a reinvention of the original design of the eighteenth-century gardens, ordered at the end of the nineteenth century by Princess Ghyka, a Rumanian aristocrat, sister of Nathalia of Serbia and, according to Bernard Berenson, a solitary, narcissistic person. After buying the estate from the d'Outreleaus, the princess set to work, composing the harmony of lights and shades, the blend of fifteenth-century abstract geometries, refined mannerist perspectives, and theatrical baroque emphasis that characterize the present gardens.

Beginning in front of a grotto dedicated to Neptune, protected by a wall decorated with geometric figurations, a grassy alley runs parallel to the building. Punctuated at first by tall cypresses, it leads from the "irrational," mannerist shade of the grotto and wood—a wood that is no longer the Ovidian forest of the Golden Bough, but a place of darkness and spells—to the neoplatonic light of a terrace, sprawling in the sun and suspended above the reassuring rural landscape. Perpendicular to the residential building, a secret garden, a kind of mystery nymphaeum, is hidden between high walls. The usual illusionist play of shells intermingled with pebbles set in the walls, the statues, and the fountain, create a dimension of sensuality.

Finally, on the southern side of Villa Gamberaia, the famous Italian gardens appear. Princess Ghyka had the layout of the ancient *pomario* (apple orchard) amplified, and the result is the present, complex design, which modulates the pre-existent orderly lines with new, variously shaped box and hornbeam hedges. The addition of a liquid note, with four fishponds replacing the former parterres, has lent more suggestion to the layout, rarifying the mighty geometries of the greenery, and the volumes defined by the topiary work. Roses and lemon pots dot the garden with their colors, culminating in the Renaissance-style exedra, which filters the visual perception of the landscape through the harmonious row of arcades that incise its rigorous volume.

Documented as early as 1398, Villa Gamberaia became a country residence for the nuns of San Martino in the fifteenth century, then passed on to Matteo di Domenico Gamberelli, called Borra, a stone dresser and father of the two famous Renaissance sculptors Antonio and Bernardo Rossellino. The next proprietors were the Riccialbanis, then the Lapis. In 1618, Zanobi Lapi, a wealthy Florentine merchant, launched the reconstruction and amplification program that was to result in the present sober, linear building. After belonging to the Corsis, the villa became the property of the noble Capponi family who, leaving the building almost unchanged, embellished the gardens with grottoes, statues, and fountains, giving them roughly their current layout. In the nineteenth century the property belonged to the d'Outreleaus who, at the end of the century, sold it to Princess Ghyka, "high priest" according to Berenson, of the cosmopolitan foreign colony that had then elected the Tuscan hills as their residence. Bought by Baroness von Kettler, the villa was severely damaged during World War II. Donated to the Vatican, it was then sold to Doctor Marcello Marchi in 1954. The works that were to restore the Gamberaia gardens to their former splendor lasted six years; they were ultimately returned to the refined, eclectic spaces Princess Ghyka had created, with the one novelty of the rose gardens and arcades, opening into the mass of the tall hedge that serves as a background, to give the gardens an airier look. This authentic reconstruction has saved Villa Gamberaia from a fate of neglect and destruction.

Documented as early as 1398, in the following century the villa belonged to the Gamberellis, the family of the famous Bernardo Rossellino. Its present aspect dates from the amplification works promoted by the merchant Zanobi Lapi, and begun in 1618. The garden was given its present major features by the Capponis, who bought the estate from the Corsis in the seventeenth century.

The grotto and secret garden transpose the mannerist poetics into the reassuring spaces of the garden.
Opposite: Opening onto the green Bramante-like ivy that closes the garden vista, the wide arches confirm the

garden's light and Renaissance characteristics. For six years, between 1954 and 1960, the garden was submitted to restoration works after the ruined villa was bought by Marcello Marchi.

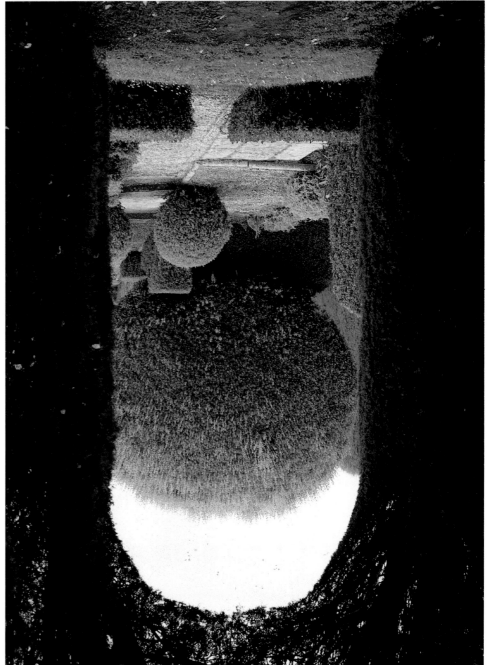

*Above: The famous Italian garden
of Villa Gamberaia reproduces the layout
of the ancient* pomario *(apple orchard).
At the end of the nineteenth century
it was reorganized by the Rumanian
Princess Giovanna Ghyka, who added
the four fish ponds where the parterres
previously lay.*

*Opposite: A solitary statue meditates,
standing on the balustrade that borders
the surrounding Tuscan countryside.*

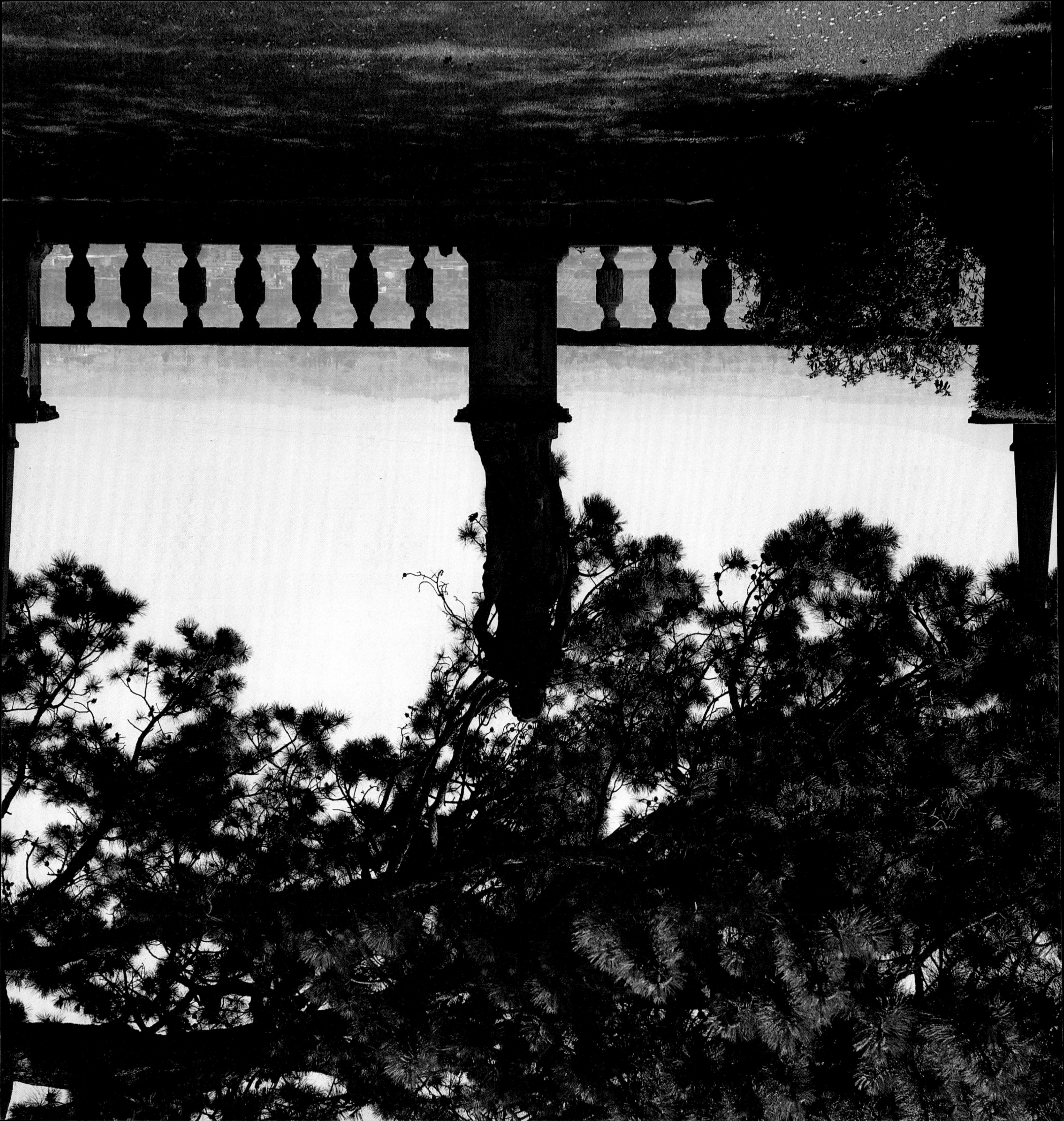

Garavicchio Gardens
Garavicchio (Grosseto)

The structural features of the Garavicchio Gardens are fairly recent, and are the consequence of a variety of interventions and influences. Situated in the southmost part of the Maremma, where the ground is dry and salty, the estate was bought in 1943 by Marquess Litta, and the first mark was left by Marchioness Maria Luisa Bourbon del Monte. She was responsible for fragmenting the gardens by means of walls, in order to protect the fragile, ancient roses and irises from the violent gusts of the north wind. This wind seems to bleach the vegetation, the meadows, the olive trees, spreading them with sand and soil, diluting their colors in dusty gradations ranging from grey to purple. Indeed the soul of this garden seems to be that of the wind, whirling around and creeping between the stones of the walls, smoothing them out and corroding them, mixing the fragrances of the vegetation and the Mediterranean maquis with the acrid tang of the Tyrrhenian Sea.

The present layout is mainly the work of Filippo Caracciolo di Castagneto, who has owned the estate since 1960, and it is divided into three terraces, the first of which is separated from the olive grove by a high wall, and sealed into a private, enclosed place that gives it a resemblance to the courtly (but at the same time domestic) conception of the medieval *hortus conclusus*. Species like verbena, *Olea fragrans* and *Plumbago*, make this first level seem a proper medicinal garden, with a counterpoint in the tender colors of *Anemone japonicae*, *Agapanthus umbrellatus*, jasmines, Buddleia, the gaudy colors of *Fuchsia magellanica*, and pervaded with the vivid smell of the lemon trees. The second level is partially paved with flagstones between which, in spring, various flowers bloom. The path to the third level is covered with a pergola leading to a lawn divided into two parts, the first of which is marked by a thin border of roses that mask a wall embroidered with datura and nicotiana. A silvery-toned mixed border, composed of *Teucrium*, *Buddleia alba*, *Senecio*, and *Ballota*, delineates the contour of the park's final section.

Since 1981, Garavicchio has been tended by Oliva di Collobiano, one of the present authorities in gardening, who has organized the area around the swimming pool. She has tried to respect the original features of the place, which have been contaminated by various experiments that have resulted in its heterogeneous aspect. It is a fond intervention that has lasted for years, and is immortalized in the pages of her book *Il Paesaggio nel Giardino* (Landscape in the Garden), almost a diary, in which Oliva di Collobiano tells about her long relationship with Garavicchio: "After that some cypresse, olive trees and parasol pines were planted, in addition to incredible quantities of cysts and roses. Today we planted two 'Madame Odier' roses, a rubiginous rose, a flowering 'Ukon' cherry-tree, ten red cysts, eight *nierembergia*, eight *sphaeralcea*, four *genista tinctoria*, eight *coronilla* and thirty prostrate rosemaries." To confirm the Mediterranean character of the garden, she has elected a palette of light blue, lavender, yellow, and various shades of gray.

The moving lights and shades depicted on the ground by the clouds, the archaeological tension of this mysterious, magic place, the proximity of the disturbing mannerist parks, spread about the Viterbo province by Farnese and Orsini, all have certainly inspired Niki de Saint Phalle in her works. Famous for her unusual "performances", during which she used to shoot at paint-saturated silhouettes, the artist has created colorful phantasmagories, inventing a supernatural world nourished by the oneiric imaginary of the subconscious, in which appear the visionary presences of women, snakes, men, and houses. Niki de Saint Phalle lives among her "creatures" in a clearing surrounded with cork-oaks, olive trees, myrtles, and mastic trees, in the woods that embrace Garavicchio, in what is called the Tarot Garden. With their quivering lines, their ironic designs—both phyto- and zoomorphic—that give them the aspect of mutants, the vivid colors of the enamels, glasses, and ceramics, their potent primitivism, these enormous sculptural totems fairly recall Gaudí's hyperbolic creations in Barcelona's Parco Güell.

There are infinite possibilities for an itinerary through this land, and no initiation way is indicated; who knows whether to start from the simulacrum of Justice, the lady of Chaos, the generator of life and order, or from the Emperor, demiurgic prince of the earthly world, moulder of matter. Or maybe the way will be indicated by the geometry of the Tower of Babel—or Maison-Dieu—topped by Jean Tinguely's metal dart, a forge of semantic confusion. Whereas the Popess, queen of night and divination, suggests a rather obscure symbology, the Sun Tarot's is clearer and more reassuring, an allegory of mystic union between heart and reason.

Annexed to the Garavicchio estate, the supernatural artistic world of the Tarot Garden is populated with Niki de Saint Phalle's undecipherable creatures.

Opposite: The Tarot Garden is dominated by the square shape of the castle, against which the Tower of Babel stands out, with Jean Tinguely's arrow emerging from its top.

Following pages: A combination of glass, ceramics, and enamels, these gigantic sculptures seem to recall Gaudí's creations, or the esoteric substance of the not-very-distant Bomarzo monsters.

Villa Lante
Bagnaia (Viterbo)

Villa Lante, at Bagnaia in the province of Viterbo, was most probably built by Vignola, who began working there in 1568 under the enlightened guidance of Cardinal Giovan Francesco Gambara, who had commissioned him. The garden of the villa is one of the most famous Italian examples of formal gardens, and according to English scholar Georgina Masson's theory, it is situated in a spatial dimension that is clearly and intentionally separated from the contiguous *barco*, a park measuring about sixty-three acres, created at the beginning of the sixteenth century by Cardinal Raffaele Riario, bishop of Viterbo, as a hunting ground.

In accordance with an iconographic program most certainly drawn up by Fulvio Orsini, a scholar in archaeology and humanities, in close collaboration with Cardinal Gambara, the two parts of Bagnaia supposedly constitute radically diversified worlds, illustrating two significant poles of the Renaissance dialectics as emblems of nature and artifice. In the park, the human intervention is more discreet, and fits the morphology of the place.

The site is an artificial mimesis of the *aetas felicior* sung by Virgil in his *Georgics*, reproducing an earthly version of Mount Parnassus, with the soft outline of its hill. This impression is first suggested by the fountain of Pegasus, the introduction to a walk across the park, guarded by the statues of the Muses standing on the elliptic curve of the wall that encloses it. It is an exquisitely Arcadian world, where the ilex copse alludes to the honey which, according to Ovid's *Metamorphosis*, gushed out under its foliage in golden days, while the fountain of Bacchus suggests a pale shadow of the wines that veined the surface of the earth in those mythical times. But the metaphor of the park has a Christian and pagan ambivalence, nostalgically pointing at the lost paradise, the biblical Eden, where the ilexes are also the trees whose wood was used to make the cross, and the acorns recall the neighboring sanctuary of the miraculous Madonna della Quercia (Our Lady of the Oak), where Gambara was buried according to his desire.

To the *barco*, a representation of the beginnings of a world permeated with nostalgic reminiscences, the gardens of Villa Lante come as a contrast. Like the passing centuries, the waters of the garden flow along in a perfect, rational watercourse system, running down the five terraces, tumultuously at first, but later to be placated in the almost motionless surface of the last fountain. These fountains have been planned in an increasing succession, and are set in a highly diversified architectural frame, with stairs, slopes, balustrades, loggias, and colonnades, to precipitate the visitor into the hyperbolic sensation of dizziness—mirror of the ambiguous essence of human artifice.

With their cubic volumes, grooved on the first floor by a blind gallery, and crowned with a turret, the small Gambara and Montalto palaces (the latter finished by Maderno in 1590 for Sixtus the Fifth's nephew, who had succeeded the cardinal) constitute the two focal points, the hinges that enclose the scenographic vista of the terraces. The first palace is decorated with an ornamental cycle depicting the labors of Hercules by

Raffaellino da Reggio and Giovanni de' Vecchi, while the second palace contains frescoes painted by Cavalier d'Arpino and Agostino Tassi in the first decade of the seventeenth century. At the top of the gardens, the extreme border of the golden age is marked by the Deluge fountain, whose waters gush out of a grotto that may allude to the fountain on Mount Aigaion, where Rhea sought refuge to give birth to Zeus, to protect him from the wrath of Chronos, his father. It is guarded by the two houses of the Muses, with Serlio-style loggias, representing the two summits of Mount Parnassus where Pyrrha and Deucalion sought refuge against the flood. From that point, the water proceeds to the fountain of the sixteen dolphins, then reappears in the next terrace among the mannerist volutes of the succession of waterfalls that flows out of a crayfish (Cardinal Gambara's heraldic emblem); then it steals into the semi-circular basin of the river divinities of the Giants. The water resumes its lively spattering in the Bramante-like fountain of the Cavea, also called fountain of the Lamps, with its luminous jets, comparable to the light of silvery candles. At the end of this fluid initiation itinerary, the water seems to lose forever its impetuousness in the quiet, peaceful liquidity of the four small lakes that constitute the square fountain of the Moors, whose transformation was ordered by Cardinal Montalto.

The surrounding nature, increasingly domesticated by human reason, is also shaped by the labyrinth of box hedges. Saint Carlo Borromeo probably disliked the atmosphere of the place: when he visited the villa, rather than perceiving it as an allegorical itinerary for spiritual elevation, he branded it a place of insidious joys, a bewitched garden of Armida filled with a thousand costly temptations. In 1653 the estate was provided with an aqueduct by its owner Ottavio Acquaviva, in order to guarantee good irrigation for the park and increase the variety of the fountains' waterworks. In 1656 it became the Lantes' property. Between the end of the seventeenth and the beginning of the eighteenth century, the frequent visits of the de la Tremoille sisters, who had married an Orsini and a Lante, resulted in a gust of French influences that brought about the modification of the parterre in the square garden after French tastes.

Acquired in 1656 on a long lease contract by Duke Ippolito Lante della Rovere, the villa, after belonging to the noble Roman family for three centuries, is now property of the Italian state. The mannerist fountain of the Moors (or fountain of the Square) carves out its niche among the French-style hedges of the eighteenth-century parterre.

From the fountain of the sixteen
dolphins, watched over by the two houses
of the Muses, the water is conveyed down
through a chain of waterfalls that begins
at the heraldic crayfish, emblem of
Cardinal Giovan Francesco Gambara,
who acquired the villa in 1568.

Opposite: The sculptures, jets of water,
and various levels of the mannerist
iconography were all too worldly for the
austere Counter-Reformation tastes
of Cardinal Saint Carlo Borromeo.

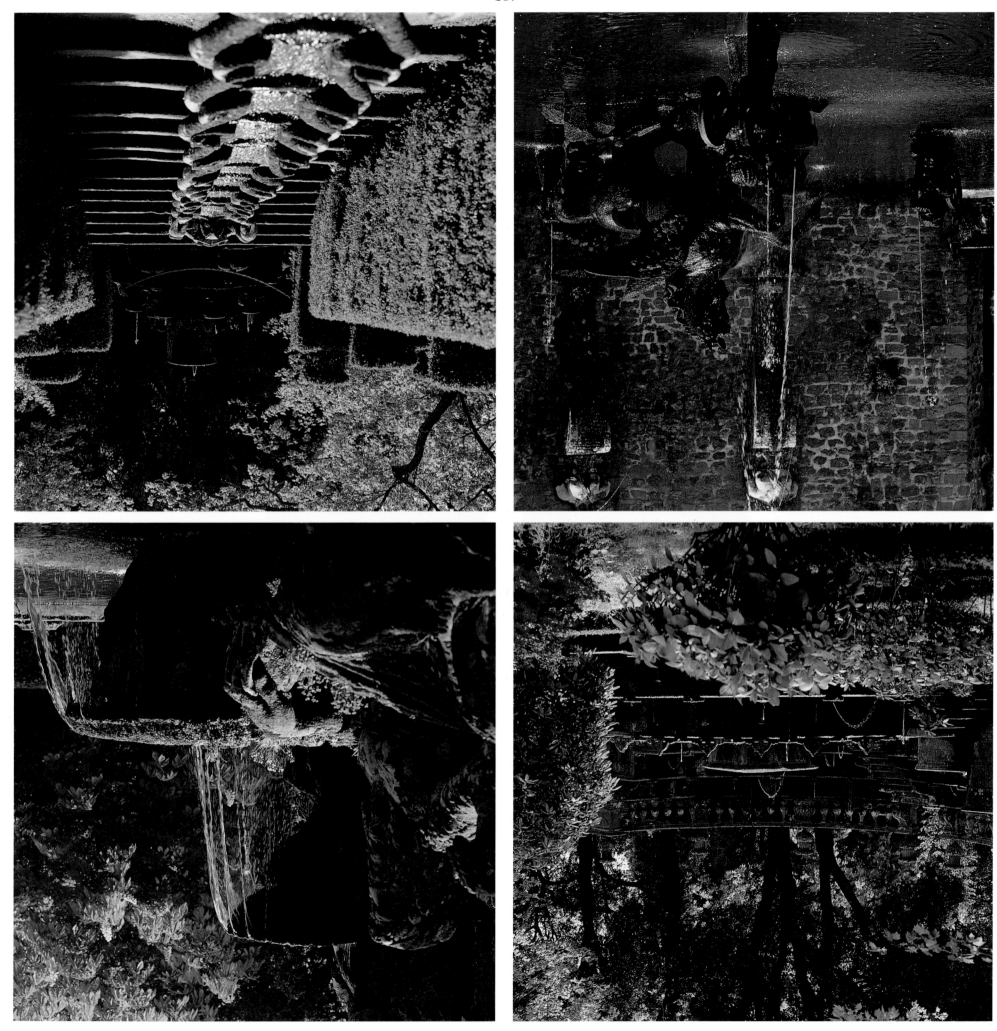

In 1653 Ottavio Acquaviva (an auspicious name), who owned the villa, had an aqueduct built to ensure better irrigation for the park. The elaborate system may have been conceived by Fulvio Orsini, Cardinal Alessandro Farnese's learned librarian.

Orsini Gardens
Bomarzo (Viterbo)

Pierfrancesco Vicino Orsini, who preferred the powder of battlefields to humanistic studies, was nevertheless a well-read man and had conspicuous friends among the scholars and the powerful of the time, among whom were his confidant Giovanni Drouet, Cardinal Alessandro Farnese, and Ottavio Farnese, to whom he was also bound by family relationship. Last but not least was the powerful Cardinal Cristoforo Madruzzo, bishop of Trent, who, although he belonged to a family that had held the bishop's throne for a century and had given hospitality to the Council, preferred sojourning in his pleasant Latium villa, not far from Bomarzo, rather than putting up with the rigorous climate of his principality. An eclectic son of mannerism, Vicino was attracted by the memories of India which assumed fanciful connotations in the collective imagination, from Rabelais' *Gargantua*, to the visionary aspect of Ariosto's poem, or Bernardo Tasso's courtly, chivalrous fable. According to Maurizio Calvesi, the initial concept for the statuary subjects might have been inspired by Tasso's *Amadigi* and *Floridante*. In an Etruria that was already dense with disturbing, mysterious ancestral presences, Orsini grafted onto the wooded landscape a garden "machinery", an anticlimax where monstrous, fantastic creatures burst out of the recesses of an impossible memory. Perhaps this was what attracted Salvador Dalí's attention, when he rediscovered in 1949 the supernatural uniqueness of Bomarzo.

Tu ch'entri qua, pon mente a parte a parte / e dimmi poi se tante meraviglie / sien fatte per inganno o pur per arte
(You who enter here, observe one thing after another and tell me if so many marvels are the result of deceit or of art).

Calvesi also writes: "Thick with tangled shadows and crepitations, the forest seems to generate the monstrous apparitions from its very womb." The medieval processional returns in the labyrinthine itinerary of Bomarzo, and it is punctuated with authentic "stations," in a continuous, convulsing alternation of dream and nightmare, of diabolical evocations and reassuring passages, deceitful or enlightening seductions for both senses and reason. As Lionello Puppi remarks, the wood, as a whole, "results in the orchestration of a figurative program of 'marvels', that condition the catharsis of landing to the overcoming of the dilemmas of 'deceit' and 'art', of oblivion and memory, of horror and beauty. . . . It asserts itself above any comparison with pre-established models, since its measure resembles nothing but itself, and therefore it is incomparable." The monumental, anti-classical, and exasperated forms—macroscopic tortoises, dragons, and turreted elephants—seem part of the place, rooted in it, and are not arranged in a symmetrical way, but look as though they were walking out of some unreal world to clamber down the steep slopes of this wooded part of the Cimini mountains. A work of the highest importance for contemporary culture, Torquato Tasso's *Gerusalemme Liberata* (Jerusalem Delivered), was printed in 1560 (the works at Bomarzo started in 1552 and ended in 1583) and its romantic and magic aspects undoubtedly provided inspiration for this bewitched wood, filled with mysteries.

The iconographic program inspired by Annibal Caro, who began staging the park's inventions in 1564, was completed and enlivened by numerous waterworks, fountains, and an artificial lake, now silent and sealed. These were a reflection of the aqueous civilization of mannerism, the scene for such original inventions as the hydraulic organ at Villa d'Este or the practical jokes at Pratolino. At Bomarzo, the clear Renaissance proportions, still in force in the neighboring gardens of Bagnaia and Caprarola, are shattered by the astonishment, the subvertion of mannerism; here, Armida reigns, and her skill can give nature's energy a favorable or a terrible turn. "You who enter, leave aside any hopes." Such is the warning engraved on the gaping jaws of the monster; but, most unexpectedly, here comes a gentler pause: inside, there is just a tiny room for banquets.

The conception of the garden has been linked with any number of names, from Pirro Ligorio to Ammannati, and a number of suggestive legends intertwine there. But the Sacred Wood, now belonging to Giovanni Bettini, remains hermetically impenetrable in its identity as an "intellectual and aesthetic Arcadia of terror".

The creation of Bomarzo—which Gustav René Hocke, in Manierismus, *defined as an "intellectual and aesthetic Arcadia of terror"—lasted for over thirty years, between 1552 and 1583. Ordered by Pierfrancesco "Vicino" Orsini, the sacred wood mirrors the eclectic literary tastes and complex personality of this son of the mannerist period. The iconographic program was conceived in 1564 by Annibal Caro, based on Torquato Tasso's* Gerusalemme Liberata.

The inventions of the park, a labyrinthine place of sophisticated deceits, corresponded to an itinerary unfolding through a range of emotions. For instance, the leaning house denies the certainties of Renaissance perspective (following page). Created by unknown artists, the sculptures and architectural elements of Bomarzo's "great scenic machinery" used to be painted in bright colors that increased their pathos. The large and small sculptures that have, almost by magic, shaped the stones found on the spot, constitute a synthesis of various antithetic cultural trends. They range from the Orsinis' heraldic bear to a dumbfounded Ceres, from the Ariostian tortoise to a winged dragon, from the echoes of classicism to the drama of the large mannerist mask.

Royal Palace of Caserta

Caserta

Ordered by Charles III of Bourbon in 1751, the Caserta Gardens are articulated upon the group of five successive waterfalls that cuts through the long central section.

In 1751, King Charles III of Bourbon commissioned Luigi Vanvitelli—son of the famous Dutch panoramic view painter Gaspar van Wittel—to build the Royal Palace and Park of Caserta. The latter, according to Francesco Fariello in *L'architettura dei giardini*, marks the most fortunate conclusion of French and Italian experiments, reorganized by a single creative mind, in a clear vision of the possibilities offered by the place. A landscape looks out to the plain and the sea on the south, and is hemmed-in by a semicircle of hills covered with thick vegetation on the north.

Caserta is probably the most delightful property in all the Bourbons' system, because it appropriates the surrounding countryside. It displays its own sumptuous affectedness, and becomes a place where "modeled" nature is celebrated in its aesthetic essence, striving to blend gradually into the free nature of the woods that cover the hills from which the whole complex seems to originate. Vanvitelli centered the garden upon the five successive waterfalls, accompanied by a double vegetal procession in the long central part of the garden, based on effects at Vaux-le-Vicomte, or influenced by the widely-circulated plates illustrating the royal parks of Versailles and Marly.

Although it is simplified compared to the original plans, the grandiose park mirrors the will for power of Charles III's happy reign; this is also reflected in the sculptures that decorate the fountains, where the hunting theme recalls the Bourbon king's great passion for this activity. Vanvitelli built an aqueduct to convey the water which animates the ramps, grotesque features, and statues, culminating in the large basin that receives the great waterfall, where the groups of Diana and Actaeon face each other. Sculpted by Angelo Brunelli, Paolo Persico, Solari, and others, they constitute the visual center of the park.

Thirteen years after Luigi Vanvitelli's death, in 1786, an English nursery gardener and botanist, John Andrew Graefer, was commissioned to draw up the plans for a new royal garden. Graefer was a product of Naples' new international cultural spheres at the end of the eighteenth century, where, in Winckelmann's wake, Mengs, Hubert Robert, Tischbein, Angelica Kauffmann, Baron d'Hancarville, Pompeo Batoni, Voltaire, the Abbot of Saint Non, Hackert, Christoph Kniep, Thomas Jones, and of course, Goethe crossed their various ways.

In her choice of architect, Queen Maria Carolina had been influenced by Sir William Hamilton—a British resident in Naples, keen collector of antiques and an admirer of Giovan Battista Piranesi's works—and his wife, the beautiful young Emma, famous for her *tableaux vivants* of archaeological taste, which Goethe himself attended in 1787 while he was staying in Naples. The queen not only wished to emulate the picturesque *Hameau*, which her sister Marie Antoinette had created at Versailles, but also to astonish her husband, Ferdinand IV, when she could present him with a tray laden with the fruit of her own garden. After Lord Banks, director of Kew Gardens near London, had granted his permission, Graefer set to work. He chose the hilly area to the northeast of the royal

park, because the water conveyed in abundance by Charles III's aqueduct made the area fertile and particularly well suited to exotic plants. Philipp Hackert's neat watercolors bear witness to the fair development the English garden had reached in 1792, and the works proceeded with the planting of a wide collection of conifers and new botanical species until 1798. The movements that resulted in the institution of the Parthenopean Republic in 1799 brought the works to a standstill, while the sovereigns fled to Sicily, protected by the British fleet.

The landscaped garden is animated by a gentle slope, ending with the arboretum on the south side. In the eighteenth century it already had a wealth of species considered rare at the time, such as the *Camellia japonica*, obtained thanks to the friendship existing between Graefer and the Swedish doctor and botanist Thunberg, who worked for the Company of the West Indies. Exotic plants from every part of the world found a home at Caserta, including Australian *Cinnamomum camphora*, *Magnolia grandiflora*, *Washingtonia robusta*, *Celtis australis*, *Cephalotaxus fortunei*, the Mexican *Pinus patula*, and the *Araucaria angustifolia*.

A small area containing Diana's fountain gives access to the garden, and the path is accompanied by the sinuous "shepherds' brook," between patches of *Chamaerops humilis*, agaves, specimens of *Yucca elephantipes*, *Nolina longifolia*, and palm trees of different varieties, among which are *Washingtonia philipera* and the rare *Livistona chinensis*. The area on which the garden develops is crossed by the paths leading westward to the monumental greenhouse, and by the brook, which runs through the garden before ending up in a lake to the south. From the mysterious "Saussurian" verticality of the tuffs—formerly populated by the spontaneous flora of Capri and the Amalfian coast planted by Graefer—one walks down in a sort of late eighteenth-century dizziness, through a dark cave, finally to emerge in the Arcadian semi-obscurity of Venus's Bath, which one can perceive through a crack in the rock. The picturesque journey continues along the banks of a small lake, where the leafy *Howea forsteriana* and a yew tree with twisted roots extend above the *exedra cryptoporticus*, carved from the rock in 1789. The archaeological play of statues, fragments, and reliefs found in the excavations of Herculaneum or Pompei, inserts itself into a context of artificially crumbling walls, and pseudo-ruins, festooned with ivy in the best Piranesi style.

A luminous, aqueous mirror covered with waterlilies, once more dominated by Aphrodite, the small lake in which weeping willows, pine trees, and the luxuriant taro are reflected is the origin of a small canal which, downstream, flows into a bigger one. There, a ruined temple stands out against the water between the sumptuous patches of palm trees, supple cypresses, and Aleppo pines. In the tropical greenhouses—botanical workshops already famous during the nineteenth century, when the last Bourbons had transformed the park into a lucrative nursery—rare specimens are kept, among which is a *Chorisia speciosa* planted in 1841.

Opposite: A fluvial allegory seems to refer once more to the abundant presence of water, conveyed to the park by the aqueduct ordered by Charles III.

Above: The will for power that characterizes the happy reign of Charles III is mirrored in the intentional union between the garden's domesticated nature and the "wilderness" of the hills in the background.

Venus's Bath is the name of the small Arcadian lake shaded by willows, pine trees, and taroes. A canal flows out of it, to merge downhill into a larger basin.

Opposite: Vanvitelli's fountains of Diana and Actaeon—with their figural groups sculpted by Solari, Persico, and Brunelli—are contrasted by the neoclassic aesthetics of the ruin and the apparently spontaneous exuberance of the landscaped garden.

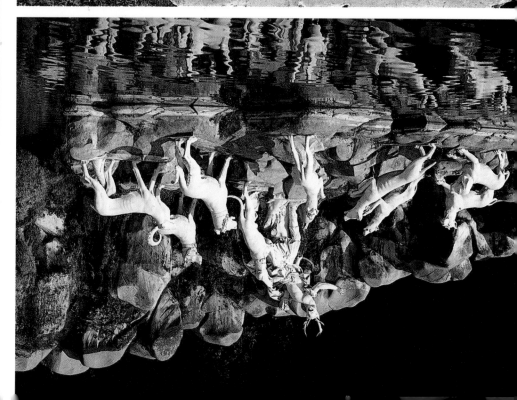

Villa Pane Sorrento (Naples)

Ruins rouse great thoughts in my mind. Everything vanishes, everything perishes, everything passes away, only time lasts. . . . I can see the marble of the tombs turn into dust and I do not want to die!

Denis Diderot's words about Hubert Robert, one of the artists the Abbot of Saint Non had commissioned to immortalize his journey in Italy, characterize the formation, at the end of the eighteenth century, of the concept of a picturesque Nature, permeated with an aesthetic meditation in front of the ruins of the past.

On the Sorrento coast, on the spot where in Augustus's time stood a villa—which may have belonged to his nephew Agrippa Postumo—stands a residence filled with pictorial suggestions, fed and enriched by the classical atmosphere of the countryside in which it is immersed. A favorite residence for writers, philosophers, and poets, between 1943 and 1945 it provided a shelter for Benedetto Croce when he fled from the horrors of war. Henrik Ibsen too, contemplating the sunset from the terrace overhanging the cliff, found inspiration for his *Ghosts.*

As in one of Jakob Philipp Hackert's or Gatel's terse, translucent landscapes, one can make out in the distance, on the cobalt blue of the sea, the outlines of Capri, Punta Scutolo, and the inevitable Vesuvius. The villa is surrounded by the exuberant life of a garden with a double charm, both exotic and Mediterranean. Ionic and Corinthian capitals, columns, urns, and impressive amphoras, mysterious nymphaeums carved in the rock to breed morays—a delicacy already recommended by Apicio in his *De re coquinaria*—bear witness to the pomp of the Roman past.

The history of the villa begins with pagan pleasures and leads to the memory of an austere women's religious community. Destroyed by the Saracens in 1558, the villa was rebuilt a few decades later by the Society of Jesus. Entrusted with the orthodoxy of the triumphant Counter-Reformation Church, the Jesuits had missions in South America and in the East, from which they brought back new botanical species. In the gardens, they began cultivating citrus fruits. Finally, in 1888, the estate was bought by the Calabrian Counts Labonia, who built the villa that can be seen today, and started arranging the archaeological remains in the park. The garden was given its final character—inspired by the stylistic dictates of the English, late romantic pictorial tradition—by William Waldorf Astor, the American aesthete who, after becoming a British citizen, was raised to the peerage in 1916.

The collections of statuary, the architectural fragments, were used again, often oddly assembled, in the thick, asymmetrical vegetation where tropical plants thrive. There are a great many species of palm trees, some of which are very rare, from the *Dasylirion*, with its firework-like explosion of tapering leaves, to the *Chamaerops humilis*, the only variety that grows spontaneously in Europe. There is also *Phoenix canariensis* and the turgid *Pinciametsa*, which comes from the Gobi Desert. And

there are gum trees, ferns, and agaves, some creepers, like the slow-growing *Ficus repens*, or the *Fuchsia magellanica*, fairly difficult to breed with its velvety leaves, and mosses, rich and soft, that creep in between the ancient stones and the blooming *Agapanthus*. In an apparently total freedom, nature breaks loose, twining among the various capitals, jars, Roman busts, and copies of more recent statues, such as Giambologna's *Neptune* who, here, does not emerge from the seething waves for which his proud, frowning eyes seem to be looking, but from a harmless, peaceful pond covered with waterlilies.

As a reminder that in such places time and space lose their frontiers to blend into an aura of blue and green, an early Christian sarcophagus immortalizing the faith of a married couple is placed near a Roman wall built with the *opus reticulatum* technique. A sixteenth-century fountain, with French marbles by Lenz, ancient bronzes and coats of arms, reached by walking under a bower of small *Banksiae* roses along the *Chamaedorae* alley, condescends to converse with the opulent bust of a Roman matron and a lanky gothic madonna. From the garden belvedere, which boldly dominates the sea like a prow rising above the blue abyss, marble herms by Alma Tadema watch as the visitor gazes into the warm sunset light or the nacreous tones of dawn softly breaking over the Sorrento peninsula. But the garden offers another refined viewpoint, even if it is less immediately spectacular: beyond the terrace overlooking the bay, Lord Astor had a wall built that runs broadside to the sea, and the wall is pierced with innumerable small mullioned windows, like so many eyes eager to contemplate such beauties. Among the soft colors of the wisteria that frames them, one may admire the sight more discreetly, like a secret guest. Rather than being overwhelmed by the whole panorama, one merely catches glimpses of it.

The strangest botanical curiosity of the garden is the very rare *Melianthus major*, obtained from the Cape of Good Hope. In this unusual case of symbiosis between the vegetal and animal worlds, an epiphytal plant—here growing on another palm tree—feeds the ants that are necessary for its life cycle with the sweet humors it secretes. The Mediterranean flora is represented by box trees, bougainvilleas, ferns, ivies, and cypresses, and the fleshy geraniums of the Amalfian coast add a gaudy touch of color. The present owners have fervently pursued Lord Astor's work and personally supervise every activity taking place in the garden. This garden that embodies the Hellenistico-Pompeian taste of the end of the nineteenth century, a mixture of the neoclassicism of the beginning of the century and romantic and realistic components, is perfectly represented by Sir Lawrence Alma-Tadema's luminous painting.

From the sheer belvedere overhanging the sea there is a splendid panoramic view on the bay of Naples. The marble herm on the balustrade was carved by Alma-Tadema.

Hemmed-in by the greenery of the cliff, the villa was built by the Counts Labonia in 1888. Henrik Ibsen stayed there, and so did Benedetto Croce, between 1943 and 1945.

Opposite: The garden abounds in dense, spontaneous vegetation, where Mediterranean plants mix with exotic species, among which are several varieties of palm trees.

Previous pages: The Chamaedoreae *alley, with its bower of small* Banksiae *roses, leads to the sixteenth-century fountain.*

Opposite and above: Architectural fragments, urns, sarcophagi, copies of classical and Renaissance statues, busts, and capitals serve as counterpoints to the opulent vegetation where ferns, agaves, palm trees, climbers, Agapanthus *and innumerable varieties of trees mingle together.*

Falsitta Gardens
Capri

"Capri, the essential island and receptacle of all the Mediterranean species," is Edwin Cerio's definition of the island in his 1939 *Flora privata di Capri*. Along with Capri's natural history, which includes at least eight hundred and seventy different botanical varieties, Cerio goes over the island's entire history, from the days of Augustus, who found here his Apragòpolis—that mythical city of the *dolce far niente*—to Tiberius's cruel, legendary amusements, after he retired to Capri for the last, wicked years of his life.

It was only in the first half of the nineteenth century that the first international tourists started discovering the charms of Capri, mainly owing to August Kopisch's and Hans Christian Andersen's writings. As Norman Douglas observes in his *SirensLand*: "it appeared, riding the wave of veneration for caves and ruins that swept over Northern Europe." Between the end of the nineteenth and the beginning of the twentieth century, in addition to being visited by mainly German and British tourists, Capri became the favorite residence of political dissidents, intellectuals, aristocratic globetrotters, pale, romantic English maidens, stout North European bourgeois, and all sorts of eccentric people. With a spirit that was often factious and missionary, they devoted their energies to creating gardens that could assume ideological or religious tones, or become places for botanical experimentation, or yet nurseries for the restoration of a real or hypothetical indigenous flora. Among the most frequent types were gardens in which the classical archaeological remains, judiciously placed in a complex scenography of exuberant greenery, reassume their original ornamental function.

Loretta Cammarella Falsitta's Capri garden, with its bold panoramic location above the bay of Naples, is a revival of the hanging garden considered a paradise of delights, which reduces everything to supreme harmony, idealization, and potent expression of the mysterious perfection of creation. The garden is reached after a narrow and difficult walk, as though to conjure up the concealed, protected threshold of the mythical Greek *gortos*. Like the garden of the Hesperides, guardians of the golden apples, situated beyond the ocean in the suspended, faraway dimension of Night, the Falsitta Gardens seem to break loose in a rarefied dimension, beyond space and time.

After walking through the compact, wooden gate, framed by climbing roses, the visitor follows an alley leading to the villa and guarded by two giant agaves, while on the right a loggia looks out onto the luminous sea and sky. Sculpted in polychromed marble, busts of Roman emperors gaze at the horizon, while the parapets overhanging the sheer cliff are crowned by more herms, heads, and sculptures.

The Tiberian flora, represented by the acanthus, the smilax—the ivy used for the Bacchants' wreaths—and *Myrtus tarentina*, mix with various species of palm trees and rare specimens of *Agave ferox*. Exuberant and intensely fragrant, the Mediterranean maquis embraces a small terrace surrounded with cypresses, with a small marble table in its center, from which there is a splendid view from Vesuvius to Ischia.

This peaceful, dignified place seems to suggest a continuous dialogue between death and life, earth and sky, the finite and the infinite, sensual enjoyment and austere meditation. A sphinx complacently supervises the sober and moderate vegetation which, if guilty of any excess, merely commits an excess of beauty.

Busts of Roman emperors of the second century seem to contemplate the sea of Capri from the open gallery in front of the villa.

210

Previous pages: A partial view of the garden and swimming pool, overhanging the sea and the port of Capri.
Above: A rare, gigantic Agave ferox *watches over the shady alley leading to the villa.*

Opposite and following page: The picturesque design of the Falsitta Garden is enlivened by palm trees, blooming bushes, herms, fragments of classical statuary, and nineteenth-century sculptures.

*Above: A secluded, meditative spot, once
more looking out on the Capri panorama.*

Villa d'Ayala
Valva (Salerno)

Valva's history begins in the year 1000, when it became a fief of Gozzolino, a lord who, according to the Norman custom, was named after the Norman tower that still keeps watch over the park. Towards the end of the eighteenth century, one of his descendants, Marquess Giuseppe Maria, decided to build a holiday residence near the tower. Strangely enough, it is reminiscent on a smaller scale of the Renaissance Buon Consiglio Castle, seat of the bishops of Trent. Appointed superintendent of all the roads and bridges of the kingdom of Naples by Ferdinand IV of Bourbon, after laying out the carriage road leading from Eboli to Basilicata, Giuseppe Maria devoted all his energies to the reorganization of his fief. Most important among the various improvements was the creation of a garden, meant to increase the pleasures of the summer residence, with the help of the best botanists, gardeners, and floriculturists of the kingdom. Thus came into being the coppice, the orchards, the alleys lined with plane trees, magnolias, and cedars, the two Italian parterres, the fishponds, the small lake, and the open-air theater that can seat one thousand spectators. This garden seems to be proud of its anachronistic character, and despite the host of mythological statues that silently people it, seems to scorn the neoclassic dream generated by the first excavations at Herculaneum under Prince d'Elboeuf's supervision, and theorized at the time by Winckelmann and the Abbot of Saint Non.

Rather than drawing inspiration from contemporaneous English landscaped gardens, or from the terse majesty of Vanvitelli's royal palace of Caserta (clearly bearing a French stamp), in its formal layout Valva incorporates stylistic features of the great Italian period between mannerism and baroque.

Situated in the Sele valley, not far from Salerno, the garden has an irregular rectangular shape, eighty-three by sixty yards, and the residential building stands on the west side. It is not reached by the usual central alley, typical of the Renaissance, but by a capricious itinerary, an invitation to pause, contemplate, and get lost in the park greenery.

On the gently sloping surface of over forty-two acres, planted with a wealth of mainly local botanical species, places with suggestive names such as Hermitage Alley, the Small Kiosk of Delights, and the Fountain of the Young Crow unfold one after another, culminating in the small open-air theater where, among the green box hedges, gods and heroes of Greek or Roman mythology peep out like alarming spectators. Perhaps in an attempt to exorcize their indifferent, Olympian presence, the local people have given the statues affectionate, prosaic names. The visitor may thus meet Big Nose, Don Luigi, or Aunt Raffaellina.

When Marquess Giuseppe Maria Valva died in 1831, the villa passed over to his wife's family, the d'Ayalas, closely involved with the supreme military Order of the Knights of Malta. In 1959, the last d'Ayala bequeathed the villa to the order to which he belonged.

The history of Villa d'Ayala begins in the year 1000 and culminates at the end of the eighteenth century, when Marquess Giuseppe Maria ordered some important renovation and reconstruction for both villa and garden. The villa was inherited by marriage by the d'Ayalas in 1831, and it was bequeathed to the Order of Malta in 1959 by the last descendant of the noble family.

Previous pages: The small open-air theater can seat up to one thousand people. Among the geometric lines of the box hedges, mythological busts peep out like alarming spectators.

Opposite and above: On the forty-three acres of the garden, abounding in indigenous botanical species and exotic specimens, the visitor frequently comes across statues in the classical tradition, to which the local people often give affectionate, prosaic nicknames.

Valea draws its inspiration from mannerist and baroque stylistic features.

Plane trees, magnolias, various species of cedars, a coppice, and several orchards compose the arboreal score of the garden.

Villa Cimbrone
Ravello (Salerno)

The magic garden occupies the whole stage. Tropical vegetation, splendid, exuberant flowers; the background is delineated by the embankment of the surrounding wall, against which some avant-corps of the castle, ornated in a rich Arabic style, lean laterally by means of terraces.

Richard Wagner's scenic indications for Klingsor's *Zaubergarten* in *Parsifal*, inspired by the composer's visit to Villa Rufolo in 1880, seem to fit perfectly the neighboring, slightly more recent Villa Cimbrone.

Not far from Amalfi—one of the four glorious maritime republics—perched on top of a cliff, Ravello perfectly suited the aesthetic ideals of the end of the nineteenth century, based upon the fanciful recovery of a fabulous past. A place where echoes of Greek and Roman classicism intersect, mixed with Arabian and Norman influences, and the opulent and legendary memories of the medieval trade with the East, Ravello became a favorite destination for the nineteenth-century Nordic traveler, desperately in search of an unreal Mediterranean character, described by Goethe, or transfigured by Wagner's morbid, transcendental mysticism. Lord Grimthorpe, a learned Scot and a keen traveler, built his exuberant garden in Ravello in 1904, on the sheer cliff overhanging the sea.

Villa Cimbrone is named after a rock jutting out into the Tyrrhenian Sea from the steep cliff of the Amalfian coastline. Free interpretation is evident right from the entrance, where a turret with gothic merlons seals the blend of Nordic flora with the Mediterranean. A long cypress alley leads from the villa to the western terrace. The surrounding wall, decked with the tendrils of a Virginia creeper, encloses a shady plane tree and wide, continental horse chestnut trees, whose presence is contradicted by the exoticism of the *Cycas revoluta* and agaves occupying big clay pots. The Moorish cloister, where twisted columns, gemel windows, and neo-gothic elements pay tribute to Landolfo and Matteo Rufolo's garden, is lit up by the colors of the Ravello majolicas, contrasting with the hydrangeas and red geraniums growing around the central well. From here, a sinuous alley winds along, lined with box hedges which, in summer, do their best to dam up the colorful sea of dahlias of various heights. The long, reassuring pergola, with its round brick columns between which bloom blue and pink hydrangeas, is a quotation from the happy period of humanism.

The various parts of the park unfold one after another, as in a suite of sumptuous nineteenth-century chambers, each with a different ornamental style. Laid out on two terraces enclosed by pseudo-Moorish balustrades, the pink garden, named after the single color of the hydrangeas, roses, and begonias that grow there, is dotted with large jars and copies of classical statues, and surrounded by pine trees beyond which loom the mountains of the southern coastline. The Arabian garden is also of Moorish inspiration and, between the fragrant roses, a strange pavilion rises, decorated with Islamico-Norman mosaics; it is bounded on the south side by the alley leading to the belvedere. From this vantage point the eye can roam the sea from Paestum to the Parthenopean archipelago.

Past the villa, enclosed in its private fence of *Phoenix canariensis*, beyond a parterre that blends the gaudy tones of *Salvia splendens*, dahlias, and marigolds with the sober mauve of the cleome and the soft plumes of the *Cellosia plumata*, the cypress alley opens up. A boundary between the full, triumphant light of the flower gardens and a mysterious, shady itinerary clinging to the rock, paved with the flagstones of the Roman consular road discovered in the excavations, the alley is covered by a bower of white wisteria, supported by white-painted columns, according to the local tradition. The alley ends up in a loggia containing a statue of the goddess Ceres, and beyond it there is another terrace with pine trees and cypresses, offering yet another viewpoint onto the blue sea. Not far away, a small, round temple with a cupola houses a bronze group representing a satyr carrying young Bacchus, to whom the small construction is dedicated. The creator of this enchanted garden, Lord Grimthorpe, was buried here in 1917. His garden is contaminated neither by the chaotic, Dionysiac lymphs, nor by the maenads' din when they celebrated the god's mysteries. It is a garden that corresponds to an ideal of balance and restfulness. It is an itinerary through the fantastic that becomes the sanctuary of nineteenth-century middle-class virtues, as confirmed by the Horatian quotation engraved on the entablature of the small temple: "Nothing is more pleasant when, after finishing your work, with your mind free from any preoccupation and your body tired of working for other people, you come back home and lie down to rest on the bed you had been yearning for."

Villa Cimbrone was built in 1904 by Lord Grimthorpe in a suggestive spot high above the sea, on the steep cliffs. The garden opens with the Moorish patio, an eclectic revisiting of Arabian-Norman architecture.

Opposite: From the Amalfian belvedere, guarded by naïvely sculpted busts, the garden opens out onto the sea, where the eye can roam from Paestum to the Parthenopean archipelago.

Following pages: The nineteenth-century picturesque feeds upon various complex stimuli: the wisteria pergola, the Arabian garden, the large jars, the neoclassic ornamental elements, and finally, the small round temple where Lord Grimthorpe is buried.

Franzin Garden
Ostuni (Brindisi)

But the garden, crushed and mortified between these barriers, exhaled unctuous, carnal, slightly putrid fragrances, like the aromatic humors distilled by the relics of some saint women; the small carnations superimposed their peppery smell upon the protocolar perfume of the roses and the oily scent of the weighty magnolias growing in the angles; and underneath them, you could also make out the tang of the mint, mixed with the childish bouquet of the false acacia and the jam-like aroma of the myrtle; and from the other side of the wall, the citrus grove sent the perfumed waves of the first, alcove-scented orange blossoms.

The sensuality of the perfumes rising from a bouquet of floral and arboreal elements, exhausted by one another's intensity, enhanced and inflamed by the summer sun, seems more than ever present in the initial pages of Giuseppe Tomasi di Lampedusa's *Gattopardo* (The cheetah). Although this passage is permeated with Sicilian culture, it may analogically recall the chaotic substance of the Mediterranean nature. And the path followed by Dino Franzin, in his search for the deeply vibrating essence of the Apulian countryside is definitely Mediterranean.

A solemn place, Apulia conceals, in the courtyards of city palaces or between the walls of the farms that dot its wide expanses, gardens that burst with colors and scents. Not far from the white houses of Ostuni near the sea, the Franzin Garden displays its beauties around a farm dating from the end of the fifteenth century, although it has been modified through the centuries. The former abode of a villein in the service of the local noble family, the building was internally restructured by Renzo Mongiardino. Like the other farms of the neighborhood, the whiteness of its thick walls is enhanced by the pink lines underlining its corners, and it is perfectly integrated in the exuberant vegetation of the garden. On the wall that encloses the garden, an endless bougainvillea unfolds its festoons and whimsical fuschia-colored volutes. This chromatic note is omnipresent in the three parts of this walled-in garden.

The owner's initial intervention has been discreet, with the enlightened help of Paolo Pejrone, one of the greatest contemporary landscape gardeners in Europe. In the new layout, ancestral elements stand out, like an enormous mulberry tree, and the ancient olive trees, with their gnarled, contorted, and sculptural trunks. The salinity of the water used to irrigate the garden has led to a natural selection of the possible varieties which, in addition to their aesthetic value, must possess a fair resistance in order to grow and thrive.

The second level of the garden houses the citrus grove, a casket for euphoriant fragrances, and an evocation of the Islamic paradises and nocturnal enclosed gardens sung by Sheherazade. Here, between the paths of irregularly cut stones, the sunny polyphony develops in the vivid tones of lemons and oranges.

The third level, built by the previous proprietor, is reached by ascending a graceful stone stairway adorned with sculptural elements. Here, the luxuriant linear segments of *Chamaerops humilis*, the delicate pale blue of *Agapanthus*, the silver green of rosemary are mirrored on the liquid surface of the swimming pool, amalgamated by the flow of bougainvillea, perpetually blooming in the outbuilding courtyard, thanks to the favorable micro-climate created by the sunny exposure and the high protective walls.

Standing out among the garden greenery, the white mass of the farmhouse dates back to the end of the fifteenth century.

The gnarled trunks of ancient olive trees stand out against the austere background of the dry stone walls.

A "fauve" symphony of bright colors is mirrored in the swimming pool, beyond the sumptuous branches of a Phoenix canariensis.

Watched over by a cypress and enlivened by geraniums, the vine-bower once more recalls the wake of classicism.

The gaudy, festive bougainvillea spreads everywhere and has become the dominant and unifying feature of all parts of the garden.

Opposite: Colors and fragrances blend— pale blue Agapanthus, *rosemary, agaves, and geraniums mix with the ivy.*

Architectural elements of the local tradition stand out against the vegetation.